A TICKET, A PACK AND A CHART

EPISODES FROM A BORDERLESS LIFE

BUZ DONAHOO

Silver Fern
Bookworks

ISBN: 978-0-9836534-1-7

Library of Congress Control Number: 2011935522

Published by Silver Fern Bookworks
263 Orange Terrace Drive,
Winter Park, Florida 32789
SilverFernBookworks.com

for Deborah O'Neal
and John Hannon,
who were with me every step of the way...

and to Geoff Benge who consistently
encouraged and assisted

"I've walked my way across Mexico,
safaried the African plain,
seen Paris by night
and Japanese kites
and most of Hemingway's Spain.

Got the money I need,
The life that I want,
A ticket, a pack and a chart.
The only thing that eludes me,
Is a certain woman's heart."

From "A Ticket, A Pack and A Chart"
Or "Happy Birthday, Buz"

≈≈≈

"Of the gladdest moments in human life, is the
departure upon a distant journey into unknown lands.
Shaking off with one mighty effort the fetters of Habit,
the leaden weight of Routine, the cloak of many Cares
and the slavery of Home, man feels once more happy.
The blood flows with the fast circulation of childhood…
Afresh draws the morn of life…"

Journal, 1856
Captain Sir Francis Richard Burton

Author's Note

All of the events described herein happened as related. This, however, is an impressionistic work based upon what is remembered, rather than retrospectively researched, therefore it is fraught with minor inaccuracies.

Various occurrences that took place on separate journeys to a particular destination have been narrated as though they happened on only one. I hope this will make it more enjoyable to read.

Some names have been altered, for obvious reasons.

Buz Donahoo

CONTENTS

FOREWORD

I was a State Farm executive in a business suit, sitting at the airport in Orlando in 2002, waiting bored and mentally cocooned for my flight when a booming, raspy voice from the nearby bank of payphones intruded in on me. I tried to tune out the voice, and then I heard the words "sled dogs" and "ice climbing" and I found myself looking over my shoulder to find the source of the intrusive, but somehow intriguing voice. A guy about my age but with a decidedly outdoorsy look was shouting into the phone at someone who was obviously (from the one-sided conversation I heard) responsible for arranging some kind of trip to connect the dogs and the ice cliffs.

I had done a little ice climbing years earlier, and a friend had introduced me to dog mushing back in Minnesota, so when the man hung up the phone I decided to approach him and check him out. (I learned much later that this man never carried a cell phone but instead relied on the old and cheap technology of the public payphone.)

"Hi, I'm Ralph Bolt," I said, sticking out my hand to shake his. "I couldn't help overhearing your conversation. I have an interest in mushing and ice climbing. What's your story?"

"Nice to meet you Ralph. I'm Buz Donahoo, and I run Condor Adventures. I'm setting up a trip to Finland for some clients who want to do a little ice climbing and sled dogging. Here, take one of my business cards."

We talked a few minutes longer and then it was time for me to board my plane. As far as I was concerned, the whole conversation had been nothing more than an interesting interlude in the dull routine of business travel.

That evening, back home in Normal, Illinois (yes, that's where I live), I emptied out my pockets and paused to look at the business card the bearded, khaki-clad guy had given me back in Orlando. The card had a website address printed on it, so I took it down to my computer and typed in the URL. I could just as easily have set the card aside and ignored it. But how glad I am that something sparked an impulse in me to go and check out the website.

"Destinations" was the first thing I saw on the website, so I followed the link. "Bonnie! This guy goes to Easter Island!" I shouted to my wife before she had any idea what I was looking at or talking about.

As a young boy I had read about Thor Heyerdahl's voyage to Easter Island, which in turn gave birth to a dream of one day visiting the place myself. And reading a few books on the island over the intervening fifty-plus years had kept the dream alive in my mind. And now, as I looked at the website, I discovered that this man I met at the airport in Orlando owned a travel company that could get me to Easter Island and make my dream a reality. I was hooked.

Bonnie, a good sport if reluctant traveler, knew of my life-long dream and instantly agreed that we should go ahead and sign up for the trip.

The rest is history. Four trips to Easter Island, the Galapagos, the Amazon, Portugal, Guatemala, the Missouri River, Egypt, and Africa, and all because I heard some guy shouting into a payphone in the Orlando airport. A world of adventure opened to me from that overheard conversation.

Over time traveling with Buz and Condor Adventures, the sites we visit have become less important than the friends we've met along the way. Each has added their own dimension to the trips, many of them to more than one trip.

And it's not just the traveling friends, but the local folk along the way. The Easter Islanders whose weddings and birthdays we've celebrated, the Maasai warriors who guarded our tents and taught us a few words of Swahili, the restaurant owners and waiters in Santiago who know Buz by name from years of serving him and his entourage, the Portuguese school kids who shared our public bus as we careened through the mountains of Portugal, the barefooted young woman in a tiny backwoods village of Guatemala waiting to greet Paula after a year or two since they last met. These are the memories that cling more tightly than the scenery of the places.

Drawing on this rich well of memory and experience, Buz Donahoo has now produced a rich tapestry that is as colorful and wide as the world. From a local coffee bar to Kathmandu, Buz's stories and anecdotes jump from continent-to-continent, country-to-country in search of those magical moments only a seasoned traveler can fully appreciate. There is much to feast on here; who knew Buz could write such wonderful prose? It is my pleasure to commend *A Ticket, a Pack and a Chart* to you. Buz Donahoo is a unique man with a unique view of how the world should be visited, which comes through strong and clear in these pages. I know you will enjoy reading them as much as I have.

Ralph Bolt
May 2011

A Stranger in a Strange Land

*My hands were in the very clay
from which the bricks were made.*

Frank Lloyd Wright

THE FIRST BUILDINGS by Frank Lloyd Wright that I *experienced* were those of the campus of Florida Southern University. You do not look at, or walk through, works by the master architect; you experience the continuous spaces as they open or close in or turn around you. The void within is sculpted. It is the reality, not the walls that define it. Even the negative spaces between structures are placed in a manner to provoke a subtle delight. The most casual observer feels that he or she is in the midst of something special. And then there is the aesthetic theme, played loudly in the form of the building, and more softly in its details.

Soon after experiencing the buildings at Florida Southern University, I called Mrs. Wright, recently widowed, at Taliesin West in Scottsdale, Arizona, home of the foundation and fellowship, architectural offices, staff and apprentice residences that bear the great man's name. After a brief conversation I was invited to come for an interview.

At that time there were about fifteen apprentices from various parts of the world living there. In all, three hundred or so had served and studied at Taliesin since Mr. Wright decided during the Depression to sustain his practice with the symbiotic help of student labor.

The complex of buildings in Arizona was located on Maricopa Mesa at the foot of the McDowell Range and, at that time, isolated from the city of Phoenix. Even today, Taliesin West is the expression of a visionary from the future. It is a desert camp.

Upon arrival I was greeted by Eugene Masselink, who had developed Mr. Wright's designs into the geometric integral ornament of windows, moveable screens, and even the table china. The master's aesthetic was first appreciated in Holland as the "De Stijl" movement, and then came back to America as Art Deco.

Eventually Mrs. Olgivanna Wright appeared, as regal as royalty. She spoke with the strong accent of her native Montenegro and in a manner that forbade dispute. She asked me some questions about myself. They seemed so few, but, as I was to learn later, she presumed an ability to perceive a lot from very little. She told of her and Mr. Wright sleeping covered by wet sheets the first summer the buildings were constructed. Talent was essential, but dedication to one's art in the face of adversity weighed heavily on her assessment of newcomers to the community. She accepted me into the fellowship and, liking my name, Wofford, said she would not change it. She had rechristened the rest of the apprentices and staff members to be called by such names as Sandrakan and Arthusa. Those who did not leave were known by her choices for the rest of their lives.

When I returned to Taliesin West to stay, a lantern-bearing apprentice led me directly to what would be my home. A hundred yards from the main complex was my eight-feet by eight-feet pyramid tent set on an eight-feet by sixteen-feet concrete slab. The dwelling was furnished with a folding canvas cot, an old-fashioned alarm clock, and some candles. Fortunately, I had brought a sleeping bag. There was a two-feet by two-feet void in the slab for a fire pit. Nearby dwellings had been developed with walls of stone supporting whimsical roofs, fireplaces and other amenities.

The days at the fellowship started with an early breakfast, and then the dancers and members of the string quartet would rehearse as the staff and senior apprentices went to the drafting room. The rest of us worked on maintenance or construction. We continually built walls, but they did not seem confining; instead, they were used only to support a structure or to subtly define spaces. Wood forms were brought up in segments to allow the placing of the flat faces of large desert stones against the inside faces. Enough concrete was then poured to cover the stones before more were placed above them. The innovative method required little skill, but the result was dramatic: gray surfaces relieved by many random areas of ocher, sienna, and umber, a "desert masonry" reflecting the natural surroundings. After a meager lunch (often cottage cheese and chili) we attended seminars on building design, ornament, and structure theory by Eugene Masselink, John Howe, and Wes Peters, all little known, even in the world of architecture, but all having influences on some of the greatest buildings of our time.

On weekends we listened to recordings of Mr. Wright's lectures at breakfast. Many guests came to stay and joined us at our daily cocktail party, including Charles Laughton, Margaret Truman, and Buckminster Fuller, along with another famous architect whose work number had become that of the bar across from his Manhattan office until, on a trans-Pacific flight, he met the woman who would turn his life around. Early one morning I watched the woman run barefoot on the dewy lawn, giggling like a little girl. I look back with amusement on a brief afternoon with Peggy Guggenheim, having no idea of her importance in the world of art.

A couple of apprentices were selected for the honor of "family servers." They would wait on a separate table for the extended Wright family and their guests. Only one person had objected to the task, because of his egalitarian principles, and only that person—Nariman Gandhi—had been granted an exception. Nari was an Indian, whose presence in our country was sponsored by Mr. Wright, who openly acknowledged him as a favorite. The Grand Old Man would chuckle and ask, "Nari, are you related to the great Gandhi?" At the "No" reply he would declare, "Well, *you* don't have to be!"

Nari admired strong, independent women, and was a close friend to some who fit that description. However, he could not tolerate the affectation of preciousness, nor mindless girlish chatter. When such arose he would unobtrusively drift away. He said that about two out of each hundred apprentices would become outstanding architects, and predicted I would be one. Sorry, Nari.

After dinner there would be a chamber music performance in the theater, followed by a film from Mr. Wright's collection. Hardly anyone owned movies, and his big reels in metal cases had been purchased from the studios. The subjects of these films ranged from the strong individual resisting society such as *High Noon,* to British comedies starring Terry Thomas and Peter Sellers, before he became known in the United States.

Those of us living at the complex were provided tickets to opening nights at the Sombrero Theater in Scottsdale. One afternoon we were guests of "Hib" Johnson at his home, which was a Frank Lloyd Wright design. So was the high rise in Bartlesville, Oklahoma, the offices of Johnson's Wax.

On Saturdays and Sundays the public was allowed entrance to Taliesin West. The apprentices provided tours, with the exception of the drafting room, a space large enough for birds to fly over the tables. There were no interior supports, the canvas roof panels were held up by gigantic beams of built-up wood members.

One stylishly dressed visitor, Laurie, took me aside to ask questions, the last being, could she come back that night to see where I lived?

She drove in with no lights and honked softly as she neared my tent. The top was down on her Porsche and soon the seats were reclined. It was good to be inside her under a black sky strewn with thousands of diamond-bright stars. She muttered a soft rhythmic chant that became more urgent just before she screamed. When I tried to stifle the sound with my palm she bit the edge of my hand. She came back about two nights each week.

What a pleasure it would be if we could conserve such feelings in a flask to sip in later times of drought.

During their first month, new apprentices were spoken to only as necessary. However, Don, a forty-seven-year-old surveyor, became my mentor and friend. He had a wry self-deprecating sense of humor. He appreciated what he learned, but was too wise to be swept into fanaticism. There was a somewhat estranged wife back in Colorado to whom he wrote occasionally. In his spare time Don would ponder ancient philosophies and teach himself to manipulate the Soroban, a Japanese abacus. Visits to town were discouraged, but we would slip away to Mag's Ham Bun in Scottsdale. Sometimes a tall beauty with broad shoulders, wide cheekbones, and hair cascading around her neck would be waiting for Don. On those nights I would return alone.

Each spring the entire fellowship packed up and moved to Taliesin in Wisconsin in a convoy of varied vehicles: vans and trucks, and Mr. Wright's fleet of rare antique autos, all painted Cherokee Red, which was his favorite color. I volunteered to leave early and drive across country with another apprentice. He drove for a while, but after a few hours he pulled over and I got behind the wheel. I had spent a summer making deliveries for an electric supply warehouse, but the GMC industrial dump truck with eleven gears was out of my league. I could not make the truck move. The other driver was appalled and ended up teaching me as we rode along. Fifteen hundred miles and four flat tires later we rolled into the Wisconsin River Valley. It was interesting to unpack the great architect's personal items, such as his collection of classical music, RCA Victor Red Labels of the complete works of Beethoven, and an old T-square with FLLW scratched into the surface. That item alone would be worth thousands today.

The large farm had belonged to Mr. Wright's aunts, who gave him free reign as to its use as a home or school. There was a large drafting room flanked by small spartanly furnished rooms quartering apprentices.

The dining room had a history. The scandals of Mr. Wright's personal life are as well known as his buildings. A servant from the Caribbean, offended by it all, locked the entire fellowship in during mealtime, except for one set of doors. He doused the exterior in gasoline, lit it, and attacked each person with an axe as they came out through the only exit. A few were killed, many wounded.

In Wisconsin there were many more areas for the apprentices to work in than in Arizona. A stone quarry yielded material for new construction, and when Nari was assigned to the quarry, he would not return in the evening. Instead, he would eat the simple meal he had brought along with a water jug, then make a bed from a couple of wide planks and sleep under a sheet of clear Visqueen until sun up. We tended the vegetables, joking about squatting in the asparagus patch. Bread was baked each day. There was always early morning work in the flower triangle road intersection, under the practical and philosophical guidance of Ling Po. He created the dramatic "night renderings," perspectives of projects in progress, thousands of tiny points of light on a slate-black background.

Kitchen duty was brutal. We would arise in the dark and work until nighttime, mostly washing an infinite number of cooking utensils and tableware. After a week of such duty, Don and I would make clandestine visits to Spring Green, the nearby farm town of about one thousand inhabitants and eleven bars. We enjoyed the company of the farmers who were pleased for a new audience for their one-liners, such as, "I'm dryer than a popcorn fart!" Don would charm Old Lil, the barmaid, while, sometimes, I would meet a local girl. They were all bovine, bulky, with large brown eyes. Having grown up with animal husbandry, they took such interaction as pleasant icing on the cake of physical instinct.

Sometimes we would stop at a roadside beer depot serving local beer and cheese. Once a demure elderly lady took our orders for drafts and pickled sausages then turned to yell, "Two drafts and two of them donkey dicks!" One such depot had been located on an out parcel of land within the farm, and its presence had rankled Mr. Wright because of its disruptive effect on the apprentices. When he was finally able to buy the place, a festive picnic was held with a violinist playing while the master burned the building to the ground.

While Mr. Wright was known for getting along with his neighboring farmers, speaking their jargon without condescension, the townspeople were another matter. They were suspicious of the strange bunch living at Taliesin. Although Wright owned the largest private collection of Japanese prints in the United States, the famous architect was in perpetual debt. He estimated that, if he had been able to pay his debts on time, he would have saved $100,000. He was in his eighties when a coal merchant struck him down in the street at Spring Green over a past due bill. Some apprentices returned that night to horsewhip the merchant.

The celebration of Mr. Wright's birthday was as festive as Christmas or Easter. Former apprentices would return (one elderly man suffered from a limp, a victim of the axe murderer). Hundreds of candles in paper cups were launched afloat across the lake and over the small dam. The dining room overflowed with guests. After toasts of praise for the new book by the editor of a major Madison newspaper, someone said, "And what about Mrs. Wright's book?" A mischievous apprentice commented that we had exhausted all superlatives in the first place, and could only repeat them more loudly in the second. The Box Projects were also presented. The design and construction of the case was someone's submission. It contained each resident's best creative effort. The interior dimensions of the container were the only restrictions. Most were architectural designs, but musical compositions, poems, paintings, jewelry, and any single creative work was accepted. When the master was alive he would candidly critique each work. Now they were presented by the artist and held up for applause.

Those who chose to spend a year, or the remainder of their lives as part of the fellowship, were unique, so much so that I never encountered another group with the qualities that set them apart. They lived true to themselves with no regard for the constraints or influences of society or their peers. They were devoid of self-consciousness. They did nothing for show or the judgment of others. They were not necessarily heroic—indeed, many were flawed—but their lives were seamless. Mr. Wright liked to say that integrity was the characteristic of being an integer, one thing throughout. And such was the case with these talented individuals leading obscure lives of which the public would never become aware. They were free, but only within the confines of their ideals. If a woman wore bright peasant skirts and ethnic jewelry, it was not for the effect. The manifestation came forth as naturally as a plant bears flowers. If there was a rule, it was do no harm. The will of others could not touch them. The sexual liaisons were as spontaneous as those of animals. Nothing was done to flaunt or display.

A little girl with new shoes crosses her dewy lawn as carefully as she can to avoid getting a droplet on the patent leather surface. Regardless of how hard she tries, the contact will be seen. Such was my exposure to the fellowship.

If there is any influence on my life as a result of the year spent in that monastic, medieval environment, I hope it is a touch of that unadorned honesty that defined those people's lives.

A Soldier an' Sailor Too

I DID NOT HAVE to go. Asthmatic since childhood, I was exempt from the draft.

But I was bored.

For a handful of friends and myself, it was the last summer prior to receiving our architectural degrees. Our days had fallen into a routine: mornings at Klissanin's Gym, afternoons at Crandon Park Beach, and nights at The Hamlet in Coconut Grove. And these activities were not without incident: the startled scream of a child upon seeing my bandaged eyes, burnt by a defective tanning machine. A young man diving in the surf between his wife's knees becomes enraged when a drunk bobs up to bite her. The surprise of a tavern dart stuck in my arm, thrown by a man whose date I had approached.

The warm summer days and nights were lethargic narrations punctuated by women, usually as exclamation points.

Miniatures from in-flight catering fueled Pan American stewardesses' parties in Miami Springs. *Five years before, I had been surprised to find that my social studies teacher, Vera Fostelle, was charming, mischievous, and only a few years my senior. She was qualified beyond training, as her brother had been a U.S. congressman for years. The girls admired her, while we boys behaved like idiots. One weekend I boasted that I would call Miss Fostelle for a date. When she answered the phone my bravado imploded and I asked her about homework instead. My friends' muffled laughter could be heard on the extension.* At one of the Miami Springs parties I recognized her, surrounded by music and laughter and wearing a globe and wing airline pin. Astonished, I exclaimed, "Miss Fostelle!" She smiled, put her arms around my neck and pulled me down for a full, deep kiss on the mouth. Leaning back she said, "Vera, Buz. Vera." It was face-saving time.

Sunday afternoons were spent at The Villas. The Twins (Tom and Ted) had an antique MG with huge headlamps, a convertible top that would stop at the Deauville position, and a loud and soft horn for town and country driving. The vehicle attracted attention as we parked near the pool. After paddle-ball we would approach men the age I am now, and referring to their young companions, ask if we could buy their "daughter" a drink. Humility was out of the question.

But we were bored.

In response to our boredom, Tom joined an Army Reserve unit, while Ted persuaded me to enlist in the U.S. Coast Guard "6x8" program with him (six months active duty and eight years in the reserves). Temporary abstinence from alcohol, caffeine, and nicotine lowered our blood pressures enough for the recruiting surgeon to accept us.

Originally called the Revenue Cutter Service by its founder, Alexander Hamilton, the Coast Guard is the oldest branch of the U.S. military, and when we enlisted, it had fewer members than the New York City police force. Before drug and immigrant interdiction became high priorities, the Coast Guard's primary duties were to protect the coasts, man lighthouses and lightships, maintain other aids to navigation, and conduct search and rescue missions. On two occasions I saw enlisted crews of three to five guardsmen under the command of a First Class Boatswain's Mate apply emergency medical treatment that probably saved accident victims' lives. They were impressive events to witness, a vivid example of the service's training emphasis on preventing death rather than inflicting it. In wartime, though, the Coast Guard becomes part of the Navy, traditionally manning landing craft during invasions. Statistics indicate an average success rate of two and one-half landings, with the "one-half" a grim joke.

The only advice we received was from a fraternity brother who had recently completed his active duty in the Guard: "Enter 'Jewish' as your religious preference. Without a Rabbi chaplain on base, they will take you on Saturday excursions to a synagogue in town and to a restaurant for breakfast." But I was naively afraid to perjure myself on a government document.

Disembarking the bus in the cold Cape May dark, I suggested we report for duty a couple of hours before the midnight deadline in order to prepare ourselves. Ted counseled spending the hiatus in a nearby tavern.

The "boot" that escorted us from the base's main gate said we would not believe what was in store for us. We stepped into the bedlam of the receiving barracks: Young men in sweat soaked fatigues, wide-eyed in confusion and fear, dropping for sit-ups or running stumbled laps around the building. There were also two lines of recruit barbers, each one slick-shaving the head in the chair in front of him, then moving up for his shearing.

In the predawn dark we were marched to Monomoy surf-boats, great, high-sided open vessels. It was easy to imagine a harpooner standing on the bow, squinting at the horizon, as the boat left the mother ship. The old guardsmen called them "pullin' boats," as in "The army has marchin', the Guard has pullin' boats." After half an hour sitting on the icy thwarts, the decision was made that it was too cold to row and so we were marched to morning chow.

The mess hall, a loud, warm refuge, allowed unsupervised companionship while satisfying a basic physical need. Two lines converged under a sign that read: "Take only what you need. Come back for seconds." Returning, we were told, "Don't believe everything you read." I recognized one of the server's drawl and mentioned to the man that my father was from Georgia. "You got a good Daddy!" he replied. Each time after that, the long spoon of this server extended to drop an extra dollop of warm comfort onto my tray.

Each day anxiety and fear eroded our aggressiveness. The only violent incident during the entire thirteen weeks happened in the shelter of the mess hall. Leaving the table, a recruit blew his nose vigorously, propelling a pulsing gob of snot over one diner's head, to land atop another's puddle of chili and rice on his divided steel tray. The offended one rose with the indignant roar of a threatened mama lion, only to be restrained by several of his messmates. It was a brief entertainment for our mealtime pleasure.

While waiting to fall-in in front of our barracks, we were allowed to smoke. When asked for a cigarette, one North Carolina boy squinted and said, "Where I come from, if I feed somebody, I fuck 'em."

Boatswain's Mate Haywood would call us to attention. We needed a hero, and Haywood was better suited for the role than most, if for no other reason than he did not enjoy inflicting punishment. Physically fit, wearing a tailored and impeccably maintained uniform, and affecting the swagger stick allowed the training cadre, he looked the perfect example of what he hoped we would become. As we stood, he would report our status to the Chief Petty Officer, who commanded Oscar Company. Mills was never there. And even the Chief knew his nickname. "Where's 'Light Duty' Boats?" he would ask. "He's on light duty, Chief," would come the reply. With one malady or another, real or imagined, "Light Duty" Mills spent most of his days in sick bay evading the hazards and drudgery of basic training, with one exception. He went with us our first day on the rifle range—just the first day. With "Ready on the left; ready on the right; ready on the firing line!" the M-1 Garands began to pop. Alas, Light Duty held the recoiling piece too close to his eye. The next day, the right cheek of his impassive face was swollen and discolored as he left for medical attention.

During the final week each company stood watch. For four-hour shifts, at fifteen-minute intervals we would punch a portable time clock at key stations located around the base. *It was eerie to walk through a darkened barracks at 4:00 AM with sixty men moaning, snoring, and farting in their sleep. Now and then one would abruptly rise to a sitting position, and, with his eyes still shut, scream out something like, "Oh, no, Mama! No, Mama, no!"* To miss a punch of the time clock meant being moved back one week in the boot camp sequence. It was the worst punishment imaginable as it meant an additional week of training, spent among a company of strangers, away from those who had become your friends. As fate, or someone's perverse sense of humor, would have it, "Light Duty" Mills was assigned to a guardhouse the size of a telephone booth at the most remote corner of the base, where the perimeter fence met at the sea. At the end of the shift, his relief found him on the floor with his feet jammed against the door. The disk he held showed that after the first punch of the time clock he had missed the following fourteen punches, effectively sending him back to the beginning of Boot Camp. I was dumbstruck with pity. Later, in Seamanship School, we heard the denouement. Seaman Recruit Mills was diagnosed as having cardiac problems that were not present at his induction. He was awarded an Honorable Discharge for medical reasons.

Bubba, a fellow trainee, spoke with a lisp. He was obsessed with becoming the best Coastguardsman ever. After lights out he would study the Bluejacket's Manual, hiding his flashlight's beam beneath his blanket. Our "display" was a proscribed arrangement of personal gear and clothing that hung, in a sea bag, from the ends of our bunks. Not maintaining the display in perfect order left the offender subject to harassment. Often we would hide some item and shout in the darkness, "Bubba, where's your boots?" or, "your fatigue pants?" or, "your chambray shirt?" This would elicit an exasperated, "Youth fuckin' guys. Youth fuckin' guys," from Bubba as he stumbled around in the dark looking for the missing item until we threw it back across the floor. We soon realized that we did not have to hide the objects; just creating doubt achieved the desired result—a diversion and a pastime.

Ted and I decided to buy a barber's kit at the PX and spread the lie that we had cut hair as civilians. After chow each night we improved our skill for a dollar per head. The only alternative was the base barbershop's service, which included mandatory "white sidewalls" two-inch wide, C-shaped shaved bands around the ears. The demand for our service soon became too great to be fun anymore, so we sold the booming business to Bradshaw. Everyone marveled that Bradshaw had passed the required recruitment intelligence test with its minimal standards. He said he had "gotten a girl pregnant," and that the small town judge gave him the choice of marrying the woman or enlisting. She declared the former choice not an option, so Bradshaw joined the Coast Guard. No one trusted him with their hair, so we bought back the clippers from him out of pity.

Ted and I were drawn to a small, closely-knit group that readily accepted us. They were all cosmopolites from the Northeast, well educated and culturally oriented. What we had in common was a familiarity with Miami, their playground. Among them was Neil, who would become Senior Sports Editor at *The New York Times* (and without whose encouragement you would not have this to read); Chuck, who would become Director of the Oppenheimer Fund; and Bobby, whose family name is on women's clothing stores throughout the nation. A coincidence almost too extreme to believe recently reunited us in a Manhattan apartment after forty-seven years.

One instructor put us immediately at ease. He said we should relax, that he was not there to make us miserable, and we should feel free to ask any questions whatsoever. Immediately a forest of hands shot up. Before calling on anyone he explained, "No, they are not putting saltpetre in your food, if for no other reason than that each person would have a different tolerance and they could not risk making anyone sick. Your impotence is a result of extreme anxiety and fatigue." Most hands went down. One day in class he exclaimed, "He's up there!" Our blank looks prompted an explanation. John Glenn was in orbit. We felt just as isolated as he was.

"Fire Fighting Freddy's" classes were dreaded, not for their rigor, but for the irresistible temptation to sleep in the warm classroom during the dull instructional films. Chief Petty Officer Frederic delighted in suddenly turning the lights on in the hope of catching a dozing, sleep-deprived boot, whom he would sentence to the standard punishment: Crawling through the hatch (just large enough to admit an adult) in the three-story boiler that was inactive that day. There the offender would spend the day scraping thick char from its interior walls. After one such day, Chuck returned to barracks with every exposed surface of his body covered in fine, black soot, except for the moist corners of his eyes and mouth.

Ted and I were accepted for the drill team, which allowed us to practice complex marching maneuvers while the rest of the company practiced P.D.U.A. (Physical Drill Under Arms—calisthenics burdened with the added nine-and-a-half pound weight of the M-1 Garand). Someone once said that America's most beautiful contributions to the world were the axe handle, the clipper ship, and the Springfield '03 rifle. The drill team carried Springfields with the wood components polished and all visible metal chromed, including the bayonet, which enhanced its needlelike aesthetic. Those on the drill team were also allowed to have their dress blues tailored. Angie, a dumpy, middle-aged Scot, measured each of us for the fitting. She was the first woman to touch us in months, and we all fell in love. She gave me a shredded Kleenex with her scent, which I carried in my pea coat for days. Our drill team exercises became meaningful when we were told that we might march in President Kennedy's inaugural parade. Nothing ever came of it.

Near the end of basic training, each company was assigned to a week in the galley. Ted had the dishwashing detail, and I was on the garbage crew, which started earlier and finished later than the others. Each trainee brought his tray to a window where he dropped glass and paper products through two counter holes, and the waste food through another that emptied into a can filling with slop the consistency of vomit. By contract, this byproduct was sold to a local pig farmer. We were supposed to prevent large pieces of meat from entering the mix, but somehow at one meal a pork bone slipped by me. The closest I came to serious trouble was when I was ordered to reach elbow deep into the slop and fish out the defiling item. The moment I considered striking my "superior" passed quickly and I yielded, swallowing pride and retrieving the bone. Each night we would scrub the cans with large brushes and concentrated detergent until they shone. Then we stacked them in a pyramid against a wall. Of course, an offending speck would always be found. The bottom corner can would then be kicked out, causing all of them to tumble, bouncing on the tile floor, and the scrubbing would begin again.

Finally we were given weekend liberties. On one of these weekends Chuck arranged dates with Vassar coeds. In Manhattan we had drinks at Trader Vic's, dinner at a famous chophouse, and later, dress blues and all, jumped into the fountain at the Seagram's building. The next morning we passed an old woman in a headscarf and threadbare coat navigating the wet pavement with the help of a rag-tipped cane. To our greeting she muttered, "Dirty, rotten sailors." On another weekend liberty we attended an esplanade concert on the banks of the Charles River in Boston.

And in Atlantic City I met Gina, a former *Playboy* Bunny. She and her friend invited us to her family's home in a wooded Philadelphia suburb. Her mother prepared bountiful Italian meals, including my first homemade pasta from raw dough. Late Sunday afternoon her brother and his buddy, on active duty in the Marines, came home. The contempt of the combatants for the non-combatants was unspoken but obvious.

While we stood at attention during graduation, the base commander announced that a chow hall Master-at-Arms had been sentenced to thirty days at the Portsmouth Naval Prison for giving the ten-year-old son of another enlisted man an unauthorized cup of ice cream.

We shipped out of Groton aboard the *Unimak*, a 311-foot training ship, bound for Nassau in the Bahamas. We were supposed to learn about being at sea by being at sea, but all we learned was to chip and paint. Daily, we were issued chipping hammers, wire and bristle brushes, wash primer, and paint. When "All Quartermasters and watch standers to chow!" came over the speakers, we knew we were next, and the tools went flying by the outside passageways and into the sea.

On the sea-lanes we passed a ship that signaled by flashing light. A reservist asked one of the careerists what the message was. "I don't know. I ain't no fuckin' Quartermaster!" the careerist replied. Ted spoke up. "I think I can read it: T...H...E...G...U...A...R...D...S...U...C...K...S."

Before we tied up at Prince George's wharf in Nassau, all hands were paid in cash. Six Chief Petty Officers immediately gathered on the boat deck to shoot craps against one of the stacks. Within minutes four were broke and two were rich.

At the end of the dock I stopped for a Heineken. Most of the crew was there. Two shipmates that we all knew to be close friends, whose physical contrast was almost comic, began to argue about whether the Coriolis Effect (the phenomenon that water draining from a basin moves in a circular motion) went clockwise or counter-clockwise north of the Equator. The slight one of the two became so angry that he hit his bulky companion on the head with a full green bottle, then blanched in fear and ran for the end of the bar and through a door that was not an escape route, only the entrance to the men's room. Sprinting back out, the slight man veered away, but not far enough to avoid a large fist driven by a ham-like forearm. As he went down, I walked away to meet my companion.

A third-grade schoolteacher had written to say that she and a friend would be spending a weekend in Nassau in the hope that we could be together. Boatswain's Mate Seabrook, in charge of our deck crew, heard about the situation and approached the Duty Officer to request special liberty for me. He was successful, and I was allowed off the entire time we were in port. The only requirement was that I report aboard ship briefly at 0800 each morning.

A British man-o-war was docked near the *Unimak, and* each morning, almost in answer to our, "Reveille! Reveille! Reveille! Up all hands!" came, "Wakey! Wakey! Wakey!" from the British ship. The laughter could be heard all over the waterfront.

One evening in Nassau, as I sat eating dinner with my third-grade schoolteacher friend, a young cockney sailor from the man-o-war with more tattoos than teeth approached our table and began to insult me. Intimidated, I was passive and cowardly. *It seems that at that time boys were allowed to enlist in the British Navy at a very young age, without parental consent, and were then divided into age groups, each under a selected bully's command. One can imagine a rural lad of fourteen having run from his father's strap returning home, hardened at twenty-four, and forcing the old man to weep and beg for forgiveness.*

When not in the bedroom with my friend, we were by the hotel pool. Rather than harboring envy, my shipmates took vicarious pride in my brief interlude. Boatswains Mate Seabrook had become champion.

～～～

As a boy visiting Northern New Mexico I had found the place dramatically beautiful, so I moved to Santa Fe. Working there for a politically oriented architectural firm, I designed the largest high school in the state, based on a grid of equilateral triangles yielding hexagonal patterns. The design won a national award. (Thirty years later, by coincidence, the son of the math department chair I had interviewed for the school trekked with us in the Andes.)

Stenzhorn and I shared an apartment in a walled compound of adobe buildings, with a bronze historical plaque by the main gate, and owned by the heiress of a Chicago department store fortune. Our personalities were opposite, but our values were the same. His habits were structured and orderly to the extreme, yet on occasion, his underlying romanticism broke through such as when he would hammer at his banjo until the ringing of the instrument could be heard the length of East Palace Avenue. He drove a red VW Beetle convertible to small towns to represent a corporation that produced business forms. I drove a red Plymouth Fury convertible, which some late nights was too wide for the rows of ancient trees that lined the avenue. I knew nothing of auto mechanics, except that with a 383-cubic-inch engine and four-on-the-floor, the Fury was fast. I would loan it to friends to race on the flat, straight two-lane airport road. Our friends were young professionals, ski bums, Mexican-Americans, and women from every walk of life, including Sarah, an administrator from the new, second campus of St. John's College. At the opening ceremony, the school's president proudly bestowed bits and pieces of the institution's historical heritage, such as the story of Francis Scott Key composing the National Anthem beneath a tree on the Maryland campus. In the address that followed, the governor of the state commented that Santa Fe was one of the Three Cities of Spain a hundred years before the Pilgrims landed on the eastern seaboard.

Fiesta had been postponed to a week later in September to reduce the number of "tourists and ebullient punks" in attendance. It began with a candlelight procession from the cathedral to the Crosses of the Martyrs overlooking the town; then *Zozobra,* Old Man Gloom, a huge effigy designed by a local artist, was burned to recorded sounds of anguish and the yearning strains of *mariachis.* The next day's parade seemed structureless to someone who had grown up with the Orange Bowl, but there was a protocol: First came a thousand Native Americans, mostly Pueblo, Hopi and Navajo, walking on bare feet. Next came the Sons of De Vargas Society on horseback, some wearing armor or moth-eaten woolen uniforms handed down for countless generations. Their ancestors left messages on Inscription Rock, now a National Monument. One, *"¡No me chingas!, Juan Dominguez,"* became a popular vulgarity. Following the Society were entrants representing schools, fraternal groups, unions, and municipalities. Next, the politicians. And then our peers in a disarray of jeeps, convertibles, and pickups, dressed in costumes of impromptu whimsy, a tub of iced beer on every horizontal surface. They were not celebrating the history of *La Ciudad Real de la Santa Fe,* but just the overwhelming joy of being alive. Private parties were announced in the pages of *The Santa Fe New Mexican,* the oldest newspaper in the United States, with cryptic nuances defining who was invited and who was not.

A more esoteric event was the Easter Keg Hunt: For ten dollars one could search out an iced barrel painted in pastel colors and hidden in an *arroyo,* and help themselves to thick slices of *cabrito,* not actually goat kid, but lamb studded with cloves and basted with chili powder dissolved in honey, as it turned over an open fire.

Georgia O'Keefe would create a special painting as a poster for each summer's opera season. We would volunteer to be ushers, servers, and bartenders, which allowed us to be in the middle of it all while watching Igor Stravinsky and others conduct their works.

By "coincidence," after the monthly formal meeting of The Old Santa Fe Society, a rogue group would venture out armed with chainsaws. Morning would find another garish roadside billboard toppled to reveal a scenic vista.

The ski basin was known for its deep powder snow. I designed a small building to house the chair lift controls and the ski patrol shelter, the first structure to bear my name.

On Sunday afternoons we would host after-ski parties. We once served our version of hot-spiced wine cooked in a new galvanized garbage can. Reaching bottom, we found it filled with two inches of curly, tinsel-like shavings. The Sabbath was dry throughout the state. No matter how much liquor was purchased on Saturday, it never lasted through the weekend. The only alternative was to drive up to Juan Padilla's grocery, honk, and when a light came on, approach his residence behind the store. *Caballero* Padilla would then sell a fifth of atrocious white port at a highly inflated price. The proceeds helped finance his candidacy for Mayor. One opponent was a likeable hippie artist, whose only campaign effort was the proliferation of Xeroxed copies of a self-portrait of his bearded, flop-hatted visage, over the slogan, "*¡Viva El Diferente!*" They both garnered appreciable segments of the vote.

One Sunday a month there was an unsanctioned match race of quarter horses on the plains. Supposedly a secret, hand-written fliers taped to Mexican restaurant windows gave the details. Many fast horses must have been foaled in the state, as the "Redneck Derby" at Ruidoso Downs was reputed to be one of the richest purses in the United States. Although there were only two entries (usually a local favorite and a mysterious unknown from out of town) the event lasted all afternoon. The crowd was mostly Mexican-American. Old men in felt hats and worn coats held bets recorded in tiny dog-eared address books. The location of a station wagon, from which Lone Star beer was sold, was whispered as covertly as if an Alcohol, Tobacco and Firearms SWAT team was poised to sweep down from the mesa. The entrants were walked around under heavy scrutiny and then led to the starting line. When a pistol was fired into the dirt, the horses would bolt down a corridor between cars and trucks parked facing each other, to cross a finish line of dime store ribbon taped to opposing fenders. It lasted less than a minute. I had lost when I sold Benny Rodriguez my MG TF, and lost again when I bet against his horse, "El Indio." I learned not to *chingas* with Benny Rodriguez.

The aspen leaves would change overnight, covering the hills with a brilliant yellow blanket that undulated from afar but up close fluttered like an infinity of tiny butterflies, signaling the "aspencade": an impromptu migration of painters, photographers, picnickers, and those who just liked to bask in the buttery sunlight.

We would hold court at round tables at the Pink Pony, or La Posada Inn, where Gentleman Jim Deavers, a former stunt rider, would mix drinks. Wanting to be king, I would pay for endless rounds. One recipient asked Stenzhorn if he could order another, to be told to, "Ask Buz." He leaned toward me and inquired, "Who is Buz?"

Those times in the Upper Rio Grande valley were some of the happiest in my life.

I was assigned to a Coast Guard Damage Control unit in Albuquerque. We were hundreds of miles from the nearest navigable body of water. Although I lived outside the radius of required attendance, the commanding officer, an insurance agent, insisted upon my attendance. I missed meetings. He refused to endorse my request for a direct commission, which was often granted to professionals. I was soon ordered to serve thirty days active duty aboard a buoy tender out of Galveston, as a punitive measure.

The nautical honeymoon was over.

Stenzhorn's pride in the New Mexico Army National Guard Officer Candidate School was contagious, and I saw it as a way out. He arranged my interview with a Master Sergeant who spoke to someone on the Adjutant General's staff. Within days I was released from the Coast Guard, enlisted in the National Guard, and immediately accepted to train as an officer.

I was given the role of Larry Shannon, the tour guide in Tennessee Williams's *Night of the Iguana*. Though the casting was prophetic, I was not to see opening night. Even in the clear skies over the San Juans, against which the Navajo judge the blue of their turquoise, clouds must sometimes form.

Christina loved a lot of men. We had spent little time together. Why she chose to place the responsibility on me, I did not know. I did know how to recognize a trap. I had saved boxes of personal correspondence, suffering under the delusion that someday someone might want to publish it. The gem was a response from John Steinbeck, handwritten weeks before he became the fifth American to win the Nobel Prize for Literature. It all went into the fire. Everything else I owned went into the trunk, except my mother's paintings, which fit on the back seat. I descended *La Bajada* in darkness, dropping down to the Mesilla Valley to Route 66...and turned West.

<center>~~~</center>

Crossing the bay into San Francisco at night seemed formidable, but I soon found the Twins' apartment on Nob Hill behind Grace Cathedral, a few blocks from the Mark Hopkins.

It was a Victorian flat, one of thousands that sprang up in the wake of the Earthquake and Great Fire. The previous year Tom and Ted had lived in a hotel, dining in a different restaurant every night. On the way to one of their favorites in Chinatown they told of their eccentric employer who, as a young drafts-man, had borrowed from friends to cover a check he sent the president of Standard Oil as payment for a requested inter-view. His design for the tycoon's home launched his successful career. At restaurants he would leave his car in traffic, give the greeter the keys, and antagonize the wait staff by demanding that tables be moved together and cleared for the spreading of building plans. He had recently died in his sleep. As soon as we sat down, the Japanese bartender exclaimed, "I read about your boss. Somebody kill 'im eh?!"

They knew the city, the blatantly famous places, and the exquisite obscure ones: Saturday chili breakfasts at Mike's Pool Hall; lunches at archaic "men's grills," where waiters with arms spread would divert women, escorted of not, to an upstairs mez-zanine; gourmet meals at restaurants along Fisherman's Wharf or a walk-away crab cocktail in a paper cup; a browse of City Lights Bookstore, the nest for the fledgling Beat Generation of writers. Sundays we drank wine in the glass pavilion at the Palace of the Legion of Honor where I met Auguste Rodin's "The Thinker," "The Call to Arms," and "John the Baptist."

A cigar-smoking lesbian I had hardly known in New Mexico came to town and invited me out for dinner. As we watched the sidewalk crowd pass by the restaurant window, she said, "See those people? Every one of them has a story. Their lives are shaped by all of the emotions: fear, love, hate, joy, and every kind of hunger. They are as complex and unique as fingerprints, and just because they cannot bring forth in words the depth of their feelings, do not think that they are one iota less than we."

We were aware of the salty legacy of the Barbary Coast: Tom was intimate with a stripper featured on the cover of a book of photographs reflecting the city. Ted took his place one night and she never suspected the deception. On a fashionable street were the flamboyant offices of the flamboyant attorney, Melvin Belli. He was the defender of Jack Ruby, who, on live television, shot Lee Oswald, the assassin of President John Kennedy. Belli's book, *Dallas Justice,* was displayed in the window. On North Beach a banner expressed gratitude for a class-action defense: "Our girls can't be topped. Thank you Mr. Belli." A small news-magazine photograph, taken from behind topless Carol Doda serving drinks to Republican National Convention delegates, made her and The Golden Condor famous. The night we went, the opening act was an unknown couple, Ike and Tina Turner. The crowd hushed as the walking bass of "Night Train" filled the room. A white, baby grand piano slowly descended from the ceiling with Ms. Doda standing on the lid, holding the stanchions, naked to the waist, with a blond braid as big as a man's forearm down her back, and grinding to the heavy beat.

I had been an apprentice at Taliesin, the Frank Lloyd Wright Foundation, after which I worked for some good architectural firms, so finding a job was easy. In the process I visited the offices of John Carl Warneke. The reception room was a long, high-ceilinged rectangle, void of decoration except for a wall covering of enlarged blue-line drawings. The focal point sat behind a large desk at the far end: a beautiful Eurasian. Marta's mother was Iberian Spanish and her father from a remote hill tribe in the Philippines. She was a contradiction. Her manner was severe, formal, and unyielding. She seemed devoid of emotion. However, what was beneath the surface seethed and smoldered.

Vatnajökull in Iceland is Europe's largest glacier. Below its surface there are active volcanoes. On occasion they break through, melting millions of tons of ice into roiling rivers. When coaxed through her brittle shell, Marta's warm moisture was more devastating than the ferocious floods that tangle steel bridges and destroy highways east of Reykjavik.

Other women appeared. I took them to our box at the Opera House to hear Joseph Krips conduct the San Francisco Symphony, on daytrips to Sausalito's No Name Bar, and overnights at Nepenthe in Big Sur.

One rainy night I gave a ride to a Berkeley student standing by the turnpike down ramp. She agreed to stop at our apartment to dry off and have a drink. *Twenty some-odd years later a letter came: "Dear Buz, Last night I had dinner with my friend, Pat. She told me of her recent camera safari and its leader. Could he be the same person who took me to meet Ted, the love of my life, who I was with for seven years..."*

In December we were invited to I. Magnin and Josef Magnum's "men only" fashion shows with unlimited complimentary drinks. I purchased for Sarah in Santa Fe a raw silk dress, with a straight belted skirt and a bolero top with three-quarter length sleeves, the color of wet wheat straw, which would go well with her auburn eyes and hair.

I agreed to attend Christmas Eve Midnight Mass with Tom and Ted. We awoke to a morning swaddled in cold, damp fog. The tree looked as if it had been designed by Picasso and decorated by Charlie Brown. We had neither family nor close friends within seven hundred miles.

A road trip was in order.

All three of us squeezed into the Twin's Alpha Romeo (the Maserati would come later) and drove to Los Angeles for a tour of Mr. Wright's houses. Each residence we visited bore the mark of the Master's hand and reflected the personalities of those for whom it was to be "home." We spent early Christmas night having drinks in a Mexicali whorehouse. We were the only patrons. The staff was melancholy and expressed grief over the tragedy of our president's death. We drove to Nogales and crossed over again for dinner at a restaurant built into caves overlooking the town. The walls of the famous place were whitewashed and supported wires that bloomed with light bulbs. The mariachis' sounds echoed through the caverns. We drove to Tempe to see the recently completed Arizona State University auditorium. It had been designed at Taliesin and I had done some of the very insignificant drafting. Our total of 18-feet, 10-inches, and 630 pounds slept in the small car in the parking lot. The next day and night we drove non-stop to arrive at Le Roy Place at 7:00 AM and report to work at 9:00.

As all the states' programs were in synchrony, I easily transferred into the California Army National Guard O.C.S. The training increased my physical strength and sharpened my leadership skills. I was surrounded by zealots who treasured heirloom insignias of high ranks, handed down from their grandfathers. They could parrot the names of battles and their military celebrities the way adolescents can concerts and rock stars. I graduated seventh out of three hundred. At the commissioning ceremony Marta pinned on my Lieutenant bars. The morning after the formal toasting, we assembled before the Adjutant General. When he announced special orders we nudged each other, anticipating deployment to Vietnam. They were only our dismissal from active duty.

Reporting to my home unit, a new Second Lieutenant without branch qualification, I was as useless as teats on the proverbial boarhog. I was told to oversee a sergeant instructing recruits in civilian clothes in the rudimentary arts of close order drill. Soon after, all junior grade officers were called in and directed to dismiss their men with the not very military orders to report back with a sleeping bag or blanket, sandwiches, and a change of underwear at 1800 hours.

Carol had just arrived and was watching television with the Twins. *She and I had become infatuated upon meeting years before. There was little age difference, although I had experienced a nervous breakdown, which interrupted my freshman college year, and had worked on a survey crew in the Bahamas, while she finished high school. On our first date she insisted that I drive the new white Ford Fairlane, a graduation present from her father. As we exited the theater, a car pulled across our path and she remarked that it looked just like hers. I had left the keys in the ignition. We drove my folks' car to her Snapper Creek Lakes home for me to meet her father for the first time. He owned the distributorship for a national oil company, and (Thank God!) an insurance agency. He was wearing only shorts and grilling by the pool. After we shook hands Carol told him of the theft. As he pushed his perfectly spherical belly against the kitchen counter, his florid face darkened to a plum color. I was silently sympathetic, less for his loss than that Carol (and her mother) expected him to like me. They left for Europe in a few days. A week later, the police called me to say they had found the automobile...completely stripped, at the bottom of a rock pit lake. Carol was a stewardess now, and when she had visited in Santa Fe her rental car was the model for the tacky macho-mobile I ordered from Lubbock, Texas.* She and the Twins were watching the news. Even before a hug she turned and said, "You won't believe what's happening in Los Angeles!"

They trucked us south to the field at Van Nuys and airlifted us out. From the plane we could see that Watts, a large part of the city, was in total darkness, except for glowing streaks of high yellow-orange flames that defined the street grid. We disembarked at an abandoned industrial arts high school, where each branch was assigned an academic wing: Infantry in the Science hall; Field Artillery, English; Armored, Mathematics, and so on. Scattered on the barren athletic field we looked like hundreds of large ground slugs as we tried to sleep. When we realized we were being fired upon, we scattered in all directions. It was reminiscent of the scene in the film *From Here to Eternity* when a Japanese Zero strafes Schofield Barracks during the attack on Pearl Harbor. None of us were hit. As we settled down there was a brief chattering of machine guns, then silence. A patrol had gone into the three story apartments across the street.

The next morning all officers were convoyed through the deserted streets. Daytime violence had almost ceased. There was block after block of burned out buildings. Hills of rotting produce spilled through broken supermarket windows and across the pavement. "4 NEGROES HAD JOBS HERE" was scrawled on the facade of a gutted laundry. The entire commercial area of the vast suburb had been destroyed. Liquor stores and appliance outlets were the first to be plundered.

Late one afternoon I surprised four sergeants passing around a pint of whiskey, against strict regulations. They snapped to attention and saluted, the highest ranking barked, "Sir! Would you like a drink, Sir?"

I commanded a platoon assigned to a central fire station, with orders to select two soldiers, armed with full clips and cartridges in their rifle chambers, to ride on the back of each truck answering an alarm as a deterrent against snipers firing on those attempting to extinguish blazes. Although instructed not to, I had to go along sometimes to avoid missing everything. None of us were hit.

After about a week an officer came to confide that we would leave the next day. The fire chief guessed what was pending and said the move was too soon.

Riding in a truck bed on the way to the airstrip, with rifles between our legs like erections, we passed a corner mail drop. A lone gunner used it as a shield while shooting at us. We were scared. None of us were hit.

Soon afterwards, I became restless. It was time to return to Florida.

～～～

Three times I have driven across the country alone, and once hitched thirty-one rides from Dubois, Wyoming, to Nashville, Tennessee, always imagining myself as the High Plains Drifter. Usually skirting the Mexican border, I would cross over for a cold

*afternoon beer in a frontier whorehouse. Two mange-ridden lions
in a steel cage by the door guarded one in Nuevo Laredo. At the
bar a barefoot young woman in a* micro minifalda *approached
me and introduced herself. "Yo soy Marta." The coincidence was
not wasted. At night I would spread my pad and bag on a state
park picnic table, then dine in silence at a small town bar and
grill. I thought I was tough, independent, and reckless. One night
the howling of feral cats frightened me into loading up and driving
another fifty miles.*

After arriving in Winter Park I received a packet of for-
warded mail containing two military documents. One informed
me that I was to receive the California State Service Medal for
having served at Watts. The other ordered me to appear before a
court martial for leaving the state without notifying the Adjutant
General. Nothing came of either.

A couple of years later I returned to Miami to work for
Thurston Hatcher, a gentleman in the best sense of the word,
and a talented architect who had also been part of the Taliesin
Fellowship. Whatever abilities I had acquired were enhanced
by my exposure to him and his associates.

I joined the Headquarters Company of an Army Reserve
Engineering Battalion just before they left for annual active
duty at Fort Benning. I was told that my assignment of commanding the Motor Pool convoy was avoided by all, and fell
to the most junior officer. I enjoyed the task and seemed to be
respected by the enlisted men. The only disciplinary measures
were requiring any infractor to guard the vehicles at parade
rest, while the others ate lunch first at the Stuckey's or Howard
Johnson's. I proffered vouchers to the Ma and Pa owners of
a motel near Ocala. They said the "coloreds" could not stay
there. As I reached across the counter to take back the chits,
they decided that we would be acceptable, if segregated. As
the Arab said upon examining the mirror, "What a difference
a little silver makes."

As Public Information Officer I was assigned still and motion picture cameramen. Warned that the Colonel was known for his lengthy, numbing morning briefings, we would stride in, ask that he pose with his staff, then leave to take photographs of soldiers posing with rifles and helmets, to be sent to such as the Palatka daily newspaper. We filmed our engineers constructing various projects around the vast camp. We searched for locations where *The Green Berets* with John Wayne was being made, but found only sets of burned Viet Cong villages; I also found the Officer's Club pool.

We took part in a morning of easy, initial paratrooper training. When told we could volunteer to add two weeks to next year's regime and take the complete course, we stood in the bleachers and roared, "Airborne! Airborne! Airborne!" *Within twelve months my wife and I had a second child, and jumping out of planes was a low priority.*

The motor pool returned a day early and I dismissed the men. That night I told the Colonel and he ordered me to call them at home and have them report back to police the armory and remain on active duty until the next night. I did not refuse; instead I performed the minor chores alone.

Our raw footage was edited by WTVJ and presented by Ralph Renick after the evening news to celebrate the Fiftieth Anniversary of the battalion.

Soon after, I received an Honorable Discharge.

Eight years had passed since we sat on the beach wondering what to do next.

Because we were bored.

Seven Shades of Blue

*Pity poor Mexico;
so far from God,
so close to the United States.*

Porfirio Díaz
29th President of Mexico

A PROPANE FLAME SWEATS the cone of layered meat in the alcove serving the sidewalk and restaurant. A knife flicks the pineapple crown and juice drips onto the small tacos. Across the narrow street, high windows in the bare, flat face of the church watch all that passes. By the door pesos are pressed into a wrinkled old palm, or used to buy comic books: Biblical or wild western, an early page invariably frames a broad-beamed nude, cringing under the leer of the malicious villain. Later, she rewards her rescuing hero with the same panorama. The plazas are called *zócolos* for the pedestals that remained after the tyrants' statues were toppled.

We depart the colonial city in a new type of car: the VW Beetle. Without guidebooks or maps, except for Sylvanus Griswold Morley's *The Ancient Maya* with its drawings of paths connecting the ruins, we venture onto the vast fossiliferous lime rock plain: the thumb opposing the geological index finger circling and defining that shallow warming pan called the Gulf of Mexico. "The Nunnery" in the ruins of Uxmal, the long

47

façade is a textured stone mosaic through which winds a huge snake, rattles erect at one end, fanged head dangling at the other: the legendary Plumed Serpent, provoker of visceral fear. D.H. Lawrence suggested that its spirit lives on in the "blood consciousness" of *La Raza,* The Race.

Our road is a fragile necklace, beaded by tiny *pueblos* around the throat of the Yucatan. Names are fraught with TZs and Xs; words never heard in the courts of Castile. People walk under my wife Chris's elbow. Profiles have receding foreheads and chins, and prominent noses, features found on the faces of every god in the Maya pantheon, adorning tombs and temples from Cobá to Copán. The Spanish did not linger to torture and massacre, as there was no gold, just as the Moroccans are safe by having no oil. The villagers have seen few from Merida, fewer from *El Norte.* We stop at a small fiesta: boys with painted faces and wooden swords, a bearded hippy orating on the square, arm raised and looking like Rodin's John the Baptist. We dine on street tacos filled with what we call "puppy parts" and chicken *mole* from crockery pots of sun-fired clay. One advisory is repeated again and again: Continue to the end of the road. There are ruins by a sea of *siete colores de azul,* a visual treasure.

All afternoon the road is deserted. At twilight it intersects another of rutted bare rock. There is no one and no signage at the intersection. We guess and turn north. We drive in total darkness for hours, potholes punctuating the monotony. Stopping at a bare block checkpoint the size of a double-holed outhouse, a boy with an M-1 attempts questions, decides we are imbeciles, and waves us on. Two more hours, another checkpoint. Well after midnight there is a glow on the horizon. Suddenly we are on the square of a town with bright lights and automobiles. On one side are first-floor arches below a lit sign: "Hotel Maria de la Luz." Ordering tortilla soup and *huevos motuleños,* we ask the town's name: Valladolid, 150 kilometers in the wrong direction.

We have come to know it well. Just far enough from Chichen Itzá to remain undisturbed, it is the commercial center for surrounding farms. The Maya rose up here in the early twentieth century. One of the huge paintings by Vargas in the Palace of the Governor shows them wielding long knives. As my Peruvian friend Lucho asks, "¿Qué es más macho, un machine gun o un machete?" The plaza is a rose garden. A family living nearby knots string hammocks used all over the region. (Hotel rooms have hooks on opposing walls to accommodate the sleeping habits of locals.) The best hotel is a historical residence converted by an owner with political connections. While traveling the country, his wife selected the best crafts available for her shop. A Winter Park merchant traveling with us returned to buy for her Park Avenue boutique. A cave on the outskirts shelters an impressive sacrificial pool.

Doubling back, we talk our way onto a military reservation, where Alex hacks away scrub to reveal a small pyramid described by Morley. I doubt if anyone has seen it since. On the coast we come upon a family living in a lighthouse; they are the only residents for miles. We sling one end of each jungle hammock from the VW doorposts, the other end to a tree. The net and fabric devices are old and crack when unwrapped. Customers of the Army-Navy store where I bought them claimed the place sold insect repellent from World War I. This was before high-tech status gear became more important than the adventure, the sizzle more important than the steak. As I roll over the seams rip and I hit the ground like a felled ox. The car shakes as my friend Alex politely attempts to stifle what Chris does not hold back at all.

At first light we walk the road until it opens to a gate of sticks in a low stone wall: a huge square compound with watchtowers at each corner, ashes from small fires upon which fragrant *copal* had been burned to honor the old gods, a pyramid perched on the brow of rock cliffs, an elevated rim along an endless coast of sand the color of unbleached muslin. These were the first mainland structures seen from the decks of Spanish galleons. Chroniclers wrote that, with a multitude of colorful banners on tall standards, the small fortress seemed so formidable that they chose to continue up the coast to make landfall at Isla Mujeres. There is no one as far as the eye can see. Iguanas bask static, the color of the gray stones upon which they lay.

Below, pastel teases the sand then runs back into a warmer shade of green, surrenders to a garish turquoise and deepens into dark indigo: seven shades of blue.

≈≈≈

At the immigration shack by the bridge over the river border, Alex is refused entry into Belize (then British Honduras). A young North American nods him outside. "It's your hair; tuck it under this," he says handing Alex a beaten T. Tyler Texas straw, the hat of choice for every farm laborer on the continent. A different person to the quick glance of the surly official, he is waved through.

A pattern quite different from that of Mexico emerges: Those who are in positions of influence, from petty officials to hotel clerks, are often openly arrogant and hostile to foreigners, an imprudent attitude for a newly independent nation hoping to attract tourism. As everywhere, children and the un-entitled are friendly and welcoming.

Houses are clad with rough boards of clear Honduran mahogany, the copper of the Philippine variety and the gold of the African. Alex and I are appalled to see this precious material used for form boards and cargo-bike boxes. Foresters walk the roads with back-hooking machetes, designed to strip away small limbs, dangling from their wrists—tools that are also used for social purposes, as the straight razor is employed elsewhere.

Entering Belize City I understand how the producers of a film to be set in an extremely impoverished African town decided to cut costs and shoot here. The streets are filthy. A toothless street preacher is ignored as, with an open Bible, he rants that we are white devils. We stay at the "best" hotel: Spartan rooms overlook the central slums that gravity, with slow deliberation, is drawing down the riverbank.

We leave on The Great Western Highway, a dirt road to the frontier, passing the bloated carcass of a mule floating in an inland canal.

Such vivid scenes have become logos in my memory's eye, such as when at the end of an early Inca Trail trek we found ourselves at the only hotel in Aguas Calientes, at the base of Machu Picchu, before it became so tourist ridden. We formed a defensive circle around our backpacks in the dining room. Between serving rounds of Cusqueña, the plump Quechua waitress took male patrons to an alcove behind an opaque shower curtain. I negotiated for a room with eight bunks and clean sheets decorated with images of Minnie Mouse and Pluto for the thirteen of us at thirty-five cents per person. At dawn I looked out a paneless window to see two large pigs mating in the mud by the railroad tracks. Dead Mule: Belize. Rutting Pigs: Aguas Calientes.

We pass Belmopan, an attempt to shift the population to a new capital, as Brazil did with Brasília in the 1950s. The latter showcases the daring work of famous international architects of the time; the former showcases grim structures with mold-streaked surfaces.

We are hand-drawn on a vehicular raft to explore ruins on a river island and then enter a country that is so exotic and colorful in the most vivid sense of the words that we have chosen to return every year since: Guatemala.

The road becomes a wide footpath and the car a small bulldozer. Saplings punch the underfloor, bushes scrape the sides, and low fronds stroke the roof. In five hours we gain fifty miles, reaming a tunnel as we penetrate the northernmost rainforest of the Americas. Turning onto a wider passage, we follow it until it ends under a grove of trees by the home of Señor Ortiz, the archaeologist, whose progeny now manage a dozen pristine duplex bungalows that are, aptly, "grandfathered in" within the national park, exactly where he then allowed us to pitch our tents. The solitude is absolute. Except for a few nocturnal bird-calls, the silence and darkness are endless.

The next day we walk through the ruins of Tikal. Suddenly giant pyramids rise above the jungle canopy. We climb the highest archeological monument in our hemisphere, holding onto roots and vines. *(A flickering super-8 reel will later show Chris at sunset in a white huipil with an embroidered yoke, reclining just under its richly ornamented crown.)*

We have our return tickets and just enough for hotel accommodation. To pay for dinner and breakfast, we offer Chris' watch to a passerby who refers us to his brother's shop. The brother tells us of another, who calls another, who meets us by the plaza. Along the way a curious couple follow the odyssey and are soon joined by three or four families chatting, laughing politely and following each conversation as their evening's entertainment.

A deal is struck: *¡Hecho!* ("Done!")

A future pattern begins to emerge.

≈≈≈

Rolling down the coast by bus, there were only Alex and a pale young man and me aboard. Mexican families celebrate Christmas night in their homes, Mexican bachelors in their whorehouses. The blackness flowed across the windows like India ink. The driver passed a bottle of mezcal to the conductor, who cut a step in the aisle to the music of the bus radio, then offered us the wheel. We exchanged looks of amazement and delight. The audacity of such an act demanded admiration and applause. However, we declined to drive.

The Midwestern lad, who knew not where to stop for the night, was enticed to join us as we disembarked at Tulum. The ruins had become known to a few of the truly adventurous, but less than a hundred a day wandered among structures appreciably unchanged since Catherwood illustrated Stephens's text with engravings of temples cleared by machetes, with jaguars prowling nearby. The few small outbuildings were *palapas,* indigenous structures of lashed sticks supporting conical thatched roofs. They appear insufferable in the sun, but the slightest breeze flows through and the dense cover insulates as it shades.

For most of my adult birthdays and the concurrent New Years', I have returned to a cluster of those buildings with every woman I have cared about, and with some for whom I cared less. Each dwelling is floored with stone and furnished with a large mattress on a platform suspended at thigh height from the roof structure. One romantic delighted in manipulating a corner rope with her foot, causing the bed to glide on a horizontal plane. She imagined the concentric rings of thatch as a choir of angels, with spine-stubs as heads and fronds as wings. Many were the mornings that she raised her voice in glory.

The shack restaurant's owner welcomed us. A widow, she had established her business by first verifying the presence of *agua dulce,* fresh water, then meeting with the Governor of Quintana Roo to negotiate transactions, the specifics of which will never see the light of day. Poor except in chicle, the territory, now a prosperous tourist destination, was the last to join the republic, with the caveat that only troops native to the region could be billeted within its boundaries.

I was surprised to see an artist from my hometown sitting at a table with her companion, a tall Englishman with blond dreadlocks. A few years before, mutual friends had asked me for help or advice on her behalf. Acting as a drug mule for a boyfriend, she had been arrested and was serving time in a Mexican jail. It was frustrating to be unable to alleviate the horror of her situation. While incarcerated, she gave birth to a baby girl. Her paintings are now in great demand. The daughter has grown to become a happy and confident woman.

We were informed that little was left to eat except *tepezquintle,* which the waitress could only describe as *carne.* When asked what type, with appropriate noises—squeals, clucks, bleating, and lowing—she could only say the animal was shot in the woods. The meat was fat-ridden but tasty, broiled in a piquant sauce. We pitched three tents on the dunes. Morning came as bright and blue as Kingman turquoise. I stepped onto the sand to see the Midwesterner standing staring, stunned and shocked by his first sight of the sea.

One year later we found him there, after returning home to divest himself of house, boat and his interest in a construction company. He had come to find the people as fascinating as their surroundings. Declaring many local dishes to be delicious, he mentioned one to be surprising: tepezquintle. *"And, you know what? It's a big goddamned rat!"*

A New Orleans painter wintered with the Punta Allen fishermen and repaired their Fiberglass boats. Either in return or from an innate generosity of spirit, they shared with him their shelter and sustenance. Returning to his Jackson Square studio, he created their portraits based upon Polaroid prints and sold them for thousands.

In the tiny town and on the beach we encountered two women. The younger, a tanned blond beauty, was friendly when alone, but aloof and indifferent in the presence of her dominant companion. Alex guessed at their proclivities, dubbing them *"Las Lenguas Largas."* One morning the younger one spread her ornate blanket just below us and made her nude way to our camp. "My mother just flew back to Houston. Would you mind if I came here to swim and do my yoga exercises?" In the words of my philosophic friend, "Even a blind hog finds an acorn now and then."

Alex met Yugi, a lighthearted and attractive French Canadian; she was the perfect anecdote to a harrowing divorce. She precipitated a hitchhiking run to the airport to change our return tickets until after the New Year. We stopped at Playa del Carmen to buy what Alex hoped would be a necessity. Our pathetic Spanish finally yielded a foil packet, its cover depicting a silhouetted couple in top hat and ball gown. The brand name: *¡Buena Suerte!* ("Good Luck!")

A holiday celebration was held on the beach: coconuts spiked with rum, a driftwood bonfire, dancing on the sand to the music of amateur guitarists.

The dawn found me held prisoner, my tent wrapped around me like a nylon straitjacket, beard aglow with the orange powder of un-rehydrated freeze-dried lasagna. After freeing myself I walked into the still, clear water as into a baptismal pool. I emerged to an epiphany:

If life can, for a moment, be this good, I will treasure such knowledge until death, hoping it will shield me from the world's hurt.

Fools Rushing In

*Mexico teaches one that perfection and timeliness
are neither always attainable,
nor necessarily desirable.*

Charlie Hood

T HERE ARE FIVE *volcanic peaks within a three-hour drive
of Mexico City. They are ideal climbs for novices, as the
challenges of high altitude, extreme weather, and steep
surfaces are all present, yet the assaults are of short duration.*

If it were not for ignorance and naiveté I would have seldom
ventured out of my zip code.

Pete Vogt and I arbitrarily resolved to climb Popocatépetl.
At 17,802 feet, its shape was that of an almost perfect cone. It
was capped with a large chalk-white glacier. (That is, until the
last major eruption, after which climbs were prohibited.)

We purchased the invaluable *Mexico's Volcanoes,* by R. J.
Secor, crampons, and ice axes. We also bought ropes. When
asked whether we wanted 11 millimeter or 7 millimeter we just
stared at each other. We were not even sure how to use them,
but we knew mountain climbers used them, and so we, too,
would need them.

Mexico City, with twenty million residents, had passed
Tokyo as the world's largest city. Eventually its population would

exceed thirty million people, though compiling accurate census data is no longer possible. The early Spanish soldiers were awed to find the Aztec capital larger than Rome at that time. An hour before landing, your airplane's shadow is already racing over the city's outlying rings of slums.

The sweet center of this vast metropolis is the Zona Rosa, an oasis of tree-lined pedestrian streets where gourmet restaurants serving international cuisine, galleries displaying large canvases, and jewelers' windows glittering with silver wrought into ancient designs abound. It is only there that I have wished I were wealthy.

The many landscaped lanes of the Paseo de Reforma sweep down to Chapultepec Park where, each Sunday, a million citizens pass through its gigantic iron gates. The crowds split around the marble monument to those who died in the U.S. invasion of 1847. Families wander through a gauntlet of vendors selling bottled juices, cotton candy, and choices of typical delicacies piled on two-hands full *chicharrón* (a blistered, fried pork skin as a platter, then splashed with fiery sauce). There is a zoo, a museum of contemporary art, a lake for row boating, and the literal and figurative highest point—the hilltop that overlooks it all. It is crowned by a castle that was the Palace of Emperor Maximillian and Empress Carlotta, whose opulent private rooms can be viewed from outside. Neither monarch spoke Spanish. Maximillian was executed by a firing squad, while Carlotta died in an insane asylum. The building once housed a military academy. Looking up at the dome over the staircase you see depicted a cadet holding a flag and falling toward you, one of those who jumped to their deaths rather than surrender to the invading U.S. forces.

Across the Paseo is the Museum of Anthropology. A roof cantilevered from one central marble pillar covers the patio there. Around its fluted surface a fountain rains down onto the perforated pavement below. The surrounding building houses a chronological display of every ancient pre-Colombian culture. The viewer passes by fan-shaped Aztec headdresses fashioned from feathers of tropical birds, around replicas of temples, and through a garden dominated by a huge, stone Olmec head. In San Francisco, my friends, the Twins, had worked with *La Espada* ("The Sword," a desirable nickname for a Latin American male), who had been on the architectural team for the museum. It had been necessary to bring soldiers in to complete construction on schedule.

A mile away, the Palacio de Bellas Artes covers two city blocks. Almost lost within is a theater. Its screen, with thousands of glass facets, is the largest work of Louis Comfort Tiffany. Depicted are Iztaccihuatl and Popocatépetl with their snowcaps facing each other across the Paso de Cortes.

It's hard to believe that there are over *one thousand* mountain climbing clubs in Mexico City, but considering that the city's population is more than that of many countries makes it easier to accept. The main club holds meetings twice a week. Pete and I attended the one that was conducted in English. The members welcomed us with an apparent concern. We left convinced that our attempt would not be child's play.

We could find few open restaurants on Sunday morning as Mexicans traditionally have breakfast at home. A few white wooden pushcarts with large wheels and scalloped trim displayed pyramids of oranges and flats of eggs. Fresh juice was squeezed into glass tumblers followed by the plop of yolks. It became my bachelor's morning meal for years after. If feeling tough, I would omit stirring the mix. Years later at the Café Express in Merida we watched a father and son served the same concoction with Fanta substituted for the natural juice. As the yellow blobs gained carbonation, they rose to the top of the neon liquid, then slowly drifted back down—a living lava light to start the day.

Leaving the pollution of the city behind, the silhouettes of Iztaccihuatl, "The Sleeping Woman," and Popocatépetl could be seen clearly through the bus window.

The bulk of "Popo" dominates the small village of Amecameca. We stopped to explore its market. The floor below the high sky-lit ceiling was a maze of vendor's stands. Animal carcasses hung in the central area. One woman offered meat samples sliced so thin her palms could be read through the sheer pink flesh. Outside under bedsheets stretched for shade, tortillas baked on a round metal surface. A wooden ladle moved through a vat of *pasole,* a stew of whole hominy, green chilies, and pork. (Old Mexicans joke that the proper ingredient is "long pig," perpetuating the theory that cannibalism was peripheral to Aztec sacrificial ceremonies.)

Within the park where the mountains are located, a road winds steadily uphill through a dense pine forest. At the top of the tree line is a lodge, a well-designed contemporary structure of massive wood beams and native stone. Within is a cafeteria; a large lounge with a circular fireplace and panoramic view of the peak and the valley; and a spacious, well-maintained dormitory.

We took note of the small Rescue Brigade building that was staffed by volunteers at all times. Two stocky Mexicans with worn equipment stopped at the beginning of the path leading up. They did not genuflect, but dropped to both knees and crossed themselves. Not child's play indeed.

Late into the night we drank and entertained two young women with stories of our adventures, (all of which had *some* basis in fact). *I have learned little, but I suspect that the vanity of most men is equal to the gullibility of some women, and these wild cards are in the deck to keep the game exciting.*

At 3:00 AM we stumbled out into the darkness to begin our assault on the summit.

We took turns carrying the eight-pound coil of rope. We had not brought the harnesses necessary for its proper use, but the burden had taken on a symbolic significance: We were mountain climbers.

Scree, a pea-sized gravel, is always deep on the surface of crater cones. Taking two steps forward while sliding one step back is work that erodes the strength and depletes the spirit. We were still fighting such footing well below the toe of the glacier when we realized that we were both dozing off whenever we rested. The mutual concern that we would fall asleep and freeze to death was unrealistic, but it was a sufficient excuse to abort our attempt. We sold the rope at the lodge.

～～～

A few months later, four of us came back and reached the top of Popocatépetl. Returning cold and hungry, we were too tired to go downstairs to the restaurant below our rooms in the village. Pulling Bill Schmidt's handy sleeping bag over me, I could not resist the bar of white chocolate by his bunk. Just as I was becoming engrossed in the plot of his paperback, he came through the door, looked around and said, "I am *so* glad I didn't bring my girlfriend!"

～～～

The next year's holiday season we returned to the city with a large group of climbers. Our hotel was charming in the best sense of the word. Most of the guests were Spanish. One older woman, a dancer from Sevilla, had lived there since a major earthquake had destroyed her home. Three of us escorted her and two friends to a tango club that, a guidebook cautioned, became rough late each night. During the show Blake bought a dozen red roses for his date. Three Mexican men were seated at a table one tier below ours. As one of them leaned forward, I noticed a shoulder holster beneath his sports jacket. He knew Blake's date, and after conversing with her, reached up and wrung all the blooms from the bouquet and dropped them on the table where they wobbled for a moment like bloody heads of small, decapitated dolls. I leaned over and whispered to Blake, "Sit down. He has a gun."

I waited at The Lodge while the others encountered a severe storm on the way up the mountain. They came down wet and excited to tell of electricity in their hair that had felt and sounded like bees. When they crouched down it would not touch them. Some had been amazed by Sergio, the Argentine guide, who strode erect up the steep ice holding his metal ice axe overhead as Lady Lightening tickled its tips.

Back in the city, invited or not, some of the team attended the hotel staff's New Year's Eve party. A few assumed that it was acceptable to take bottles as they left. At 4:00 AM I was paying our bill at the reception desk when there came the staccato chatter of high heels on tile. I turned to see the dancer, in a harem costume, playing finger cymbals as she moved across the lobby floor. She invited me to return to spend a weekend, which I did. She suggested that we stay at another hotel, which we did. Only later did I learn that she was the mistress of the hotel manager, Michael Valle.

～～～

A couple of years later the following conversation took place:

"This is Buz Donahoo calling from the United States. I would like to reserve three double rooms for six guests for the nights of April 16, 17, 18, and 19."

"I am sorry, but we do not accept groups."

"We have stayed there with a larger number in the past."

"I'm sorry, but this is a family hotel."

"Well, can't you treat us as though we were a family?"

"We cannot honor your request."

"Just let me speak to Michael Valle!"

"This *is* Michael Valle…*Mr. Donahoo!*

Bailey's: A Cautionary Tale

Some of them write to the old folks for coin,
That's their ace in the hole.
Others have girls on that old tenderloin,
That's their ace in the hole.

They'll tell you of money they've made and they've spent
And flash a Missouri bankroll.
But their names would be mud,
Like a chump dealing stud
If they lost that old ace in the hole.

Ace in the Hole
Dave van Ronk

Two brothers from New England blessed our town with Bailey's, a bar and restaurant that gratified social appetites we did not know we had. You could come with friends, business associates, lovers (current or anticipated), or sit alone at the bar tended by engaging professionals, neither tough old hacks nor preoccupied students. Saronged waitresses, mostly divorcées, lent glamour while maintaining a dignity that demanded reciprocity. Areas within were defined by levels and by low barriers of wood, polished to reveal the grain in the Japanese manner. The only decoration was a host of winged Balinese goddess dolls hanging from the ceiling like huge dragonflies. The conception of every aspect was artful, thus seeming effortless. The mood was "easy like Sunday morning," though incidents and accidents sometimes occurred: the lighting of a joint at a table, or the deliberate overturning of a champagne bucket.

Our meandering streets lined with ancient oaks beside placid lakes grew around the nuclei of winter visitors and a small liberal arts college that once had a polo team and is highly regarded in the isolated world of academe. It is a beautiful place to return to, especially if you depart often. A very small but highly visible segment of the populace, while not exactly pretentious, is certainly self-conscious. They flock like damaged birds to a particular café, and gaze over their shoulders more than at their companions, wishing it was all more like Aspen or Park City or Carmel. Their cosmetic surgeons thrive. Glossy magazines show them what they must buy. And they yearn with all their hearts to be thought of as cool... which makes them the natural prey of anyone who can make them feel special.

And so into Bailey's saunters a gregarious and jocular yogurt distributor. Several shout, "Yo Pop!" to which he retorts, "YO MOMMA!" to the delight of many. Dom for the table; Yo Pop buys. A big gratuity for the server; Yo Pop pays. His Porsche keys for the servile pretty one; he hands them over (whispering about a substance in the glove box). How could you not like him, basking in the reflected attention bought by his generosity, not costing you a penny?

The owners allow him a monthly tab. How could they refuse? Big spender, lavish tipper, regular customer. Other establishments follow. Friends extend loans: "Why not? He's good for it." His payments start to come later and later, the debts growing as imperceptibly as grass grows.

His tagalong lawyer plans an extravagant party. The lawyer pays, to be reimbursed later. "Why not? He's good for it."

One morning, his employees become concerned by his absence. At his house the blinds are down and the curtains drawn. The Porsche is not there. By evening his offices are aflutter with narrow yellow tapes.

I imagine him, a few days later, arriving at a resort in the Rockies recently publicized as "the place to be," joking with the gas station attendant and gleaning information. After driving around for hours he parks in a lot filled with SUVs in neutral colors. At an umbrellaed table he reads the local newspaper in its entirety. Nearby sits a young couple. The woman displays David Yurman. The man displays a studied arrogance. He asks some questions. They invite him to join them.

After awhile he offers to buy a bottle of Dom.

MARYLOU

I wish I didn't know now,
what I didn't know then.

Against The Wind
Bob Seger

WHEN I FIRST saw Marylou, she was handing out melon liqueur samples at an organizational meeting for a jazz festival, working for the advertising agency promoting the event.

Marylou was beautiful. She was also kind, affectionate, and mischievous. She was intelligent, but her depth of knowledge was limited from having been raised in a gated community by parents who had read only magazines since college. On their mantel was a photo of a younger she on the knee of a golf celebrity who later became somewhat of a local philanthropist. Her image had graced the covers of several fashion publications. Her deepest secret was having posed for a rather modest nude shot, taken from behind, for a prefabricated tub and shower manufacturer.

I found her agency offices and she agreed to have lunch. She lived with a boyfriend so self-absorbed that he paid no attention to Valentine's Day and little to her birthday. One night we met in the mall parking lot. She did not raise her head when the security cart passed with its flashing yellow light.

Her boyfriend soon moved out of their condominium that her father owned.

Marylou's Indian sister-in-law taught her to completely depilate her body, including the down on her forearms, to hold her hair over burning incense, and to rub her bare lips with a bark irritant to amplify their natural color.

Our brief romance became a friendship and she came to work for me. The sun shone each time she walked in, even on the rainiest days. Eventually she quit to pay visits to a friend at his beautiful home in Hawaii, which she loved. On his tables were small bowls of cocaine (which she liked a lot).

One day she called to invite me to Park Plaza Gardens for dinner and to ask my advice. She wanted my opinion as to whether she should agree to take small quantities of contraband on her trips. Upon my knocking over a water glass, two waiters stepped up to lift the tablecloth corners and whisk away the entire setting, flowers and all. (That I remember this so vividly indicates how provincial I was.) She had been assured that "if something happens" a formidable attorney would be provided for her defense. I told her not to consider it, the risks were arguably low, but the penalties could be draconian. She said she would decline.

One morning her friend, who had replaced her in my office, was late coming in to work. This was so exceptional that I called, to be asked if I had seen the newspaper. Marylou had been arrested as she boarded a flight to Hawaii with packets taped under her dress. Her parents were there for the flight departure. The "formidable attorney" did not appear. A friend of her father, whose specialty was real estate closings, represented her.

Marylou spent three years in Alderson Federal Prison Camp. "Squeaky" Fromme of the Charles Manson "family" was incarcerated there at the same time.

Marylou wishes she didn't know now what she didn't know then.

Requiem for a Risk Taker

*He's a walking contradiction, partly
truth and partly fiction...*

He's a Pilgrim
Kris Kristofferson

FILLING THE LIVING *room of the small home, we listened
to the usual generic platitudes of grief. Then stories came
forth that defined the man. Only those who knew him could
believe them.*

An economic recession allowed us long coffee mornings at
East India Ice Cream Company. The group swelled or shrank
daily, but there were those who formed its core: An inventor who
had forfeited his position with a military contractor for moral
reasons, eventually selling his bell-activated, wireless answering
device to an international telecommunications corporation. A
talented, charismatic architect, who along with his wife, attracted
a cult following of young professionals mimicking their every
affectation. A graphic artist whose beautiful creations ranged
from a mythical horse as a college logo, to a peacock on municipal manhole covers.

Leo was the wild card, the loose cannon, the free spirit. His
large forehead was bracketed by brows, arched in fixed surprise,
over eyes alive with a fierce fanaticism, fostering the image of

a mad monk. It was an impression he encouraged, wearing a hooded cassock to costume parties and murmuring benedictions in perfect Latin. He spoke several languages and dialects and could play classical piano compositions by ear. He delighted in the company of intelligent women, the challenge of complex ideas, and the excitement of being at risk.

The story goes that he had been a radio operator and then First Mate on Windjammer cruises. He "cancelled" his contract on the Pacific Rim and made his way across Asia and Europe, returning home having circumnavigated the Earth. He would enlarge and embellish such tales, but the truth of those few in which I was a minor participant was sufficiently bizarre as to require no exaggeration.

Wanting to think of myself as adventurous, I was vulnerable to Leo's every dare. Thus he enticed me to join him to find the "Bimini Wall," a submerged phenomenon of dubious archeological validity, yet fascinating to those who have a penchant for unsolved mysteries.

Within days we were flying across the Florida Straits, low enough for fishermen to wave up at the passengers above as they were transported in a cabin decorated by murals of black palm trees backlit by garish sunset-inflamed beaches. The climate was controlled by rows of 8-inch oscillating fans suction-cupped to the bulkheads. Chalk's Ocean Airways remains the oldest airline in the United States. My father had told of surveying on Biscayne Bay for the dredging of Government Cut and seeing Mr. and Mrs. Chalk with a cashbox at an umbrellaed table on MacArthur Causeway.

I had been to Bimini in the Bahamas before. The tiny main island is shaped like the pounds sterling symbol (£), the long leg of which narrows at one point to fifty yards of buckling sidewalk with sand sloping to the bay on one side and to the open ocean on the other. Each morning at the island's southern tip a crowded ferry, waves lapping over her gunwales, brings workers the short distance from South Bimini. Nearby, the seaplanes lower their wheels and labor up a ramp to a small parking lot. A block down was Brown's Hotel, operated by Ozzie Brown and brothers, with a small, exciting bar always awash in music and laughter. A dockside bronze plaque honored New York Congressman Adam Clayton Powell, a native son. When a Life reporter asked this slickster what his reaction was to a long list of allegations that led to his censure and the loss of his legislative seat, he answered, "Nobody's perfect!" Farther down, across the street, stands The Compleat Angler, made famous by Ernest Hemingway, the modest lobby adorned with photos of the writer standing beside quarter-ton Marlins. The passive resistance of resident landowners to selling their plots for consolidation effectively blocked large-scale development. Many were such as Pearl, who served her conch chowder to five tables at dinner behind a picture window displaying hand crocheted items, an elementary school crayon drawing, and a King Conch shell that had not been overly abused by the diver's hammer. Prevalent among those who lived there was also a sense of satisfaction (some would call it laziness), that also deterred exploitation. However, Bonefish Billy and Bonefish Sam and Bonefish Isaac would meet in the predawn darkness for breakfast at the only open diner while waiting for their hung-over clients to appear. At the Northern tip, weeds grew through web-like cracks in a tennis court attended by rusting earthmovers. It was nearby that a third-grade teacher and I (and a crowd of Bahamians) attended a dance at an unpainted block building with no doors or windows in the openings and only the sky for a roof. Chubby Checker played while we won First Prize: two pair of boat shoes donated by Manny's General Store. Within a year I returned to Bimini on my honeymoon. In front of his place of business Manny, a large black man in a crisp white shirt, shouted as we passed, "Hey, Tweestconetestant! How you bean, Mon? Tweestconetestant!" "What is he saying?" my new bride quizzed. "I don't have the slightest idea," I said with a shrug.

Our arrival afternoon in Bimini was passed with Leo and I on the beach, swimming in water with the tint of lime Kool-Aid. Leo, naked on the sand, claimed his belly scar was the exit wound for a loop of intestine removed to curtail obesity. Taking offshore bearings from a poorly printed publication, we found a formation ten feet below the surface on the ocean floor that could be imaginatively construed as manmade. We snorkeled up large stone chunks from the bottom and laboriously wrestled them into our open boat.

Our return flight to Florida overshot the channel. As the plane banked, the reflection of its underside raced across the glass façade of the *Miami Daily News* building. At the trailer/terminal, a receptionist told the pilot there had been a dozen angry calls.

The U.S. customs officer at the Chalk's trailer, a diver, allowed us to clear customs with a wet burlap sack full of large stones shimmering with sea life. In my driveway we sledgehammered the stones to fit small drawstring bags stenciled with "Bimini Wall." We packed the bags, along with copies of Certificates of Authenticity fashioned from stick-on letters and borders, into rigid cardboard cylinders illustrated with an undersea photo, and then shrink-wrapped them in clear plastic film.

A few gift shops gladly took the item on consignment and offered them for sale.

Not one was sold.

～～～

Leo agreed to purchase a Norwegian built sailboat that had seen better days. George, a man of Greek parentage, and I agreed to crew on the new boat on a shakedown cruise up the Intercoastal Waterway from Miami to Titusville. An excited voice announced on the telephone that the deal had been struck. The boat's seller and her girlfriends were planning a party with us as honorees. Early the next morning we would set sail for a revised destination: Bimini again. The festivities went late and we cast off from Dinner Key Marina at just after noon. What should have been a daylight crossing would go deep into the night.

Well after dark a severe line squall came up, throwing eight to ten-foot swells. The old, ill-equipped Scandinavian lady began to come apart at her seams. Before Leo could reef the mainsail it began to rip away from the boom. The tiller started splitting at the gudgeon where it joined the rudder. I tried to hold it together with both hands as rain pounded down. We were taking on water when George complained about his soaked cigarettes. Leo's head swung toward mine. We were unable to see each other's eyes, but an unspoken thought passed between us: *"He has no idea..."* Now and then across the dark, running lights would flicker. We had no radio, but Leo began to signal s.o.s. with a small flashlight each time we crested a wave. I had learned Morse code in Coast Guard Seamanship School, but for all I retained, it could have been Sanskrit. Hours later, a vessel miles away seemed to come closer. One of her lights flashed as Leo read: "A...R...E...Y...O...U...I...N... T...R...O...B...L...E...C...O...M...I...N...G...T...O...W... A...R...D...Y...O...U." Her great mass slowly came alongside our foundering sailboat. In the beams of the ship's searchlights a silver thread shot high above us, then followed the weighted monkey's fist as it miraculously hit our deck like a shot. The thin heaving line was hauled in pulling with it the rope, thicker than most men's arms, which we secured to our bowline. Tiny figures high above ran forward with the other end of the rope. I was certain that we would swing under the vessel's fantail and be ground up by the churning screws. We weren't.

Then came the task of climbing the Jacob's ladder up the six-story side of the ship, a Herculean task as by then we were each as weak as a newborn. Rough, heavy blankets were wrapped over our shoulders. Those of us who chose whiskey instead of orange juice to revive ourselves lurched for the lavatories.

The Seventh District Coast Guard headquarters was notified of our predicament and soon a ninety-five foot cutter came
as close as she could to the ship. The Coast Guard crew tried to
shoot a line over to us. But their small search and rescue cutter
bobbed like a cork, while the mammoth Poseidon we were now
on moved up and down lethargically, making their job all but
impossible. We each spoke with the Coast Guard Commander
in Miami and agreed to stay aboard ship. The cutter pulled away
with our sailboat in tow. We later learned that Leo's pride and joy
capsized and sank on the way in. The ship's radio officer patched
me through by radiophone to my girlfriend. She responded to
my narrative of salvation in a voice slowed and thickened by
emotion. I looked forward to her welcome.

The vessel we had ended up aboard was the *Mary,* a Greek
dry bulk super freighter, returning empty from Odessa, Russia. I
seem to remember her capacity as 750 thousand metric tons. As I
have a crippling indifference to numerical values (like primitives
who know only "few" and "many") that figure may be grossly
erroneous. The captain was an island Greek, in my opinion, the
noblest people on earth. His family was of the soil rather than
the sea, and he was proud to have a command. The crew was
of scattered origins from Brazil to Bangladesh, and Leo could
converse with most of them.

At daylight, I stood on the edge of the dark bottomless can-
yon that was the cargo hold. Hatch covers of folding panels, wide
as I am tall and long as the ship's beam, were fitted with gears
and cables that groaned as the lids toiled to cover the void below.
The great superstructure moved as imperceptibly as growing
grass across the Gulf of Mexico, bound for Galveston, Texas.
Well before arrival, customs officers came aboard to make sure
there was not one single grain of wheat in the holds. We tossed
our passports into a basket for an Immigration officer to col-
lect. George offered a Florida driver's license and a business
card from his shopping mall flower kiosk. The Coast Guard

verified his U.S. citizenship. While we waited, the crew mused about various ports around the world. We were surprised at the consensus that the two most vicious and dangerous ports were New York City and New Orleans. We left the *Mary* with the crew busy buying used going-ashore clothes from metal-banded bales on the dock.

For months afterwards, on chance encounters, some friend would exclaim, "I thought you were dead! Lost at sea!"

Leo paid the remaining balance of half of the price of the sailboat. He then wrote an article for a free shopper's newsletter, accompanied by a photo of him treading water. The lakeshore in the background tended to diminish the dramatic impact. At the time battery advertisements as cartoons decorated the back covers of men's magazines and comic books, telling of lives saved from Grizzly bears, avalanches, and other catastrophic dangers, by the dependability of their batteries. Leo submitted his story, hoping that the maker of the batteries would compensate for his boat losses in return for publication rights.

One day a package arrived from the company. It contained no message, just an empty plastic flashlight that retailed for about $1.47.

≈≈≈

The Little Professor was a successful bookshop. Leo wanted to open one around the corner and call it *The Professor Little,* furnished with a chess table, a full teapot, and a stock of very used books donated to hospitals, prisons, and military bases, which they had been persuaded to re-donate to Leo. The landlord, a notorious automobile dealer, reneged on the lease.

By then I was planning and guiding Inca Trail treks each year. To raise money to meet us in Peru, Leo spread the thousands of volumes on his lawn, covered them with polyethylene sheets during the week, and offered them for sale each weekend. The proceeds were just sufficient to take him as far as Panajachel, Guatemala.

There is only one such place as Panajachel. It lies on the shore of Lake Atitlan, which Aldous Huxley called the most beautiful lake in the world. There is a long switchbacking road down to the town that reveals with every turn a more dramatic view of the body of water surrounded by extinct volcanoes that are some of the highest peaks in the country and which plunge to a depth some say has never been determined. Panajachel is a boomtown populated by wealthy expatriates, Maya in native dress, shopkeepers with only first names, and old hippies still looking for the bus station. Around its perimeter are twelve Tzutuhil villages; the more remote, the more intact their culture.

A local bar owner let Leo use his oven to bake and sell pizza between nine and midnight each evening to earn some extra income.

Leo postponed returning to Guatemala City to renew his visa until it was a month overdue. The immigration officer ordered him to go directly to the airport. At the departure gate he wrote post cards to two women. One was a Pulitzer prize-winning journalist whom I admired. Each card was different: One bore a photo of the lake, the other a photo of the market at Chichicastenango. The messages were different (except that they both expressed his delight in the anticipation of seeing them again). The names of the recipients were different—the addresses, erroneously, were the same.

One woman remained unaware of Leo's return. To the other, his return became of no importance whatsoever.

≈≈≈

"…geologists, radio operators, divers…must be willing to use weapons to protect life and property." So read the want ad that ran in the Orlando Sentinel.

Leo and I met with the former Texas law enforcement officer at a suite in a chain motel. He said that he had financial backers and an agreement with the Peruvian government allowing him to mine gold in the jungle for five years and then turn the operation over to the nation. Customarily precious metals mined in Peru could only be sold to the government at lower than the current world market price. The exception was jewelry. Even now shops place beautifully crafted treasures on the pan of a triple-beam scale to yield bargain prices.

Leo accepted a position as radio operator for the venture. Finally, after many delays, the operation began. A few months later a co-worker said his wife had notified him that the flow of his paychecks had run dry. Other workers found their situations similar. Leo and a compatriot went to the Palace of Justice (a misnomer) to file a complaint against their employer. He was brought in, but after money allegedly changed hands, it was the plaintiffs who were arrested. During the convoluted legal maneuverings that followed, Leo met and became friends with the U.S. Consul. And when the diplomat had to go to Lima for a medical crisis, Leo was named Acting Consul in his absence.

The following is taken from the article "The Two Souls of Peru," published in *National Geographic*, March 1982:

> American adventurer Leo Little was about to leave Cuzco for a couple of months of gold prospecting in the Madre de Dios jungle near Puerto Maldonado. He'd been back in civilization only briefly, but that was enough.
>
> "You get used to it out there, somehow. Heat, snakes, bugs, wild animals, thieves and con men and murderers, every possible danger and discomfort you can imagine. But you're your own man. If you survive, you've got yourself to thank for it.
>
> "A while back I was working at a gold camp out of Puerto Maldonado, deep in the jungle. There are dozens of big gold camps out there right now, and thousands of small pick-and-shovel operations. It's a genuine gold rush, Peruvian style.

"Well, one night at dinnertime a huge storm suddenly blew in out of nowhere. Winds must have been a hundred miles an hour. You could hear the trunks of 150-foot trees snapping…like explosions. One tree fell right on the dining table with 50 men inside. Three killed right off, 12 injured. Two more died that night. Took several days to get survivors out of there to a doctor.

"Another time I was out alone sawing a log for the sluice. The chain saw I was using slipped and hit my leg. Sliced it clean open. I'd have bled to death if I hadn't sewn my own muscle and skin together with a needle and thread. No, sir, it's no place for folks who want the easy life. But at least you don't get bored."

"But at least you don't get bored."

When I asked our driver to take the newly arrived river expedition members around the Plaza de Armas before going to the hotel. I was amused but alarmed to see *"¡El Condor Regresa!"* in rough red brush strokes over the arches. There was no question as to who painted the words. However, the secret police had harsh policies toward civil disobedience because sixty percent of the land area was controlled by the Shining Path.

Leo showed me the restaurant he owned with a Peruvian partner. Each night he posted transcribed BBC Falkland Islands War reports on the door. Each morning they were covered with graffiti.

I met his bride from U.C.L.A., who was in Cuzco doing graduate studies on Quechua song patterns.

I never saw him again. But this I know to be true: Leo lived his life without a whine or a whimper.

The Roof of the World

*But you have been kissed on the cheek by clouds
the rest of us have only seen from below.*

Gloria Bliss

THE RECENT SUCCESS *of a Condor Adventures climbing
team on Mount Kilimanjaro provoked memories of my
first time on the great mountain. The next six times I
summited, we had the services of porters and cooks, which were
comforts indeed. Just-told tales from the returning group of vic-
torious climbers indicates that conditions on the route up have
changed little in the twenty-three years since I first strapped on
my pack at Marangu Gate.*

The conversation of the other half dozen or so groups in
the dining room was subdued. We all sat in silence, not from
fear, or even worry, but from a vague uneasiness that we might
have taken a step too far.

Most of us were Floridians, flatlanders: two brothers, a
printer and a claims adjuster, a director of a tanning lotion
corporation, an architect, a designer, a dental hygienist, an
accountant, an insurance agent and his wife, parents of three
adult daughters, and the hostess of a television series, who
would one day direct the CBS filming of our camera safari.

They were bold or they would not have been there. They were there as novices to attempt an ascent of Mount Kilimanjaro, at 19,340 feet the highest point on the continent of Africa; a great mass of volcanic earth with one-hundred-foot thick ice for frosting. And it was there to test our strength of will.

We were going to follow the Normal Route on our ascent: five nights and six days on the mountain, with one of the days free for rest and acclimatization to the altitude. Guidebooks for those who would not even consider such a climb sometime call it the "Tourist Route." Climbing manuals do not call it that, and those who have been to the top and down often call it "The Hardest Thing I Have Ever Done."

The quiet dining room was part of a small hotel, also the home of a British widow and her friend. The surrounding plantation no longer produced coffee, but catered to climbers from all over the world, providing the two elderly women with an income sufficient enough to cover their basic needs. More importantly, it covered the needs of a staff who had attended the family for years and who now fired the hot water furnace, cleaned the rooms, and, in spotless clothing, served our hearty family-style meals on linen table cloths set with heavy silver scratched with age but polished to a deep glow.

The only other nearby accommodation was at a larger hotel, frequented by package tours. The place was bland and dull.

The day before we had walked the one road into the village of Marangu, past small Anglican churches with brilliant bougainvilleas spilling over fences and crowds, mostly women and children, leaving to walk to their rough homes tucked behind small cornfields. The children wore starched white tops and the women kimono-style dresses of "Kenya cloth" in complex patterns of strong colors that, by contrast, darkened the brown of their skin. The bars were one-room buildings with bare openings. In the yard behind one such establishment stood a large barrel filled with *pombe*—banana beer. We each scooped the

thick liquid up with a gourd dipper and raised it to our lips. It
looked like pancake batter and smelled like vomit, but it was not
too bad. The alcohol came through as what wine connoisseurs
would call an *undertaste*. Barefoot men in ragged clothes sat on
the thresholds. We were five miles away from the squalor of the
main road. It was a pleasant walk among the friendly people of
the Chagga tribe, independent owners of small farms, prosperous by the standards of Equatorial East Africa.

We were actually *on* the mammoth mountain, but it was
no more perceptible than being on the sphere of the earth. The
only thing that looked like a mountain was the crater rim: black
with a white cap, four days away and about four miles above us.

Riding in from Arusha, all we could see of the mass was a
slate blue slope on one end of the horizon and an opposing slope
on the other, the rest hidden by a wall of gray clouds. Then a
knob of bright chalk appeared above, so high we had to tilt our
heads back and look up. And we were still twenty miles from
the mountain's base.

The Chagga move freely across the border between Tanzania
and Kenya on the lower slopes of Kilimanjaro. The frontier
doglegs around the mountain, as it was deemed fair for Queen
Victoria to have Mount Kenya on her side, and Kaiser Wilhelm
II to have Kilimanjaro on his.

Every African on the park staff is Chagga. Their apprentice-
ships begin with five years as porters, then five years as guides, and
five years as hut caretakers. Having moved up successfully, they
are qualified to join the Rescue Brigade, an elite corps housed in
special barracks, wearing special uniforms, and trained to cope
with any emergency.

We loaded into an open truck and rode through Marangu
to the smiles and shouts of all we passed. *There is now a hospital
along the road with an* AIDS *wing of windowless rooms locked from
the outside.* We turned at a waterfall to pick up a large group from
the other hotel. A man with the logo of a large tour company

on his shirt asked which of them would like to lead. We were appalled. One lad was carrying a guitar. *We were to see a drove of them, halfway up, turned around and heading down. The boy was dragging his instrument. A porter held a pretty young woman upright. There was a loose articulation to her joints as though the tendons had failed.*

At the park entrance I argued, cajoled, and begged for us to ascend without porters, hut stays, and cooks. The officials said that it was mandatory for us to sleep in the huts. For that we would later be thankful. Our packs weighed about twenty-five pounds each. Every item had been weighed or checked by catalogue description. Cardboard cores were removed from toilet paper rolls, handles broken off toothbrushes. Only the essentials were on our backs, including one powdered, freeze-dried meal per day, and a lightweight tent, which we did not need. We were required to pay hut fees, entrance fees, daily fees, and rescue fees.

The paved trail soon turned to gravel, then a footpath, and then a maze of roots as we slowly gained altitude. The afternoon was spent moving through a green cloud forest slaked by streams and waterfalls. Suddenly Mandara Hut appeared in a clearing. It was a huge A-frame structure. Its massive beams supported a first floor with an open porch and a spacious interior enclosing picnic tables and a wood burning stove obscured by wet clothes hanging like flags of many colors. Upstairs was a long narrow passageway between two rows of double bunks. Invariably, anytime a hut was mentioned, a Tanzanian would interject that they were built by Sweden. Effective and inexpensive international good will. Smoke rose from the caretaker's buildings as the dinners for other teams were prepared. We heated water in canteen cups over Sterno cans and poured it into the foil pouches. The red sauce meals (chili, lasagna, spaghetti) were good. Some, such as the "Oriental Delight," could induce vomiting.

The sunset view from the porch was magnificent.

Edwin, one of the caretakers, came by with another man who was emaciated, silent, and would not make eye contact. He said, "He made love with men. He is sick. Can you help him?" I thought, "Oh, dear God, if I only could!" The caretaker said he would have *griffa* when we came down if we wanted some to smoke.

The next morning we left the trees to rise through rolling terrain covered with unfamiliar flora such as the giant groundsel. At Horombo Hut we rested for two nights and a day, to acclimate to the altitude, which is a matter of the body's vital systems adjusting to oxygen deprivation. At Horombo that life-supporting element is a much smaller percentage of the ambient air than at sea level. A bulletin tacked to the hut door warned of the dangers of cerebral and pulmonary edema. The former is an increase in the brain's intercellular fluids, causing headaches and nausea; the latter, a filling of the lungs with liquid similar to drowning. Both can be fatal. The cure is to go down. The sign also warned that the young are more vulnerable in that they are more aggressive and inclined to move upward faster than is prudent. Under the structure lay three stretchers with handles at each end and a bicycle wheel mounted to the center. That evening I paid a caretaker to prepare a meal for us. I remember homemade soup, a baked potato, and some unusual meat, undoubtedly surplus from one of the big companies making their way up the mountain. What luxury!

At dawn we started across The Saddle, a barren lunar landscape totally devoid of plant life. Although the incline was shallow, the height would not allow more than a slow, deliberate pace. To the right appeared Mawenzi, a fumarole blown out as a lesser eruption, eroded to sheer spires of bristling rock. Our guides said climbing it required "cords."

Porters coming down, regardless of the weight of their burdens, would call out greetings in Swahili: "Jambo!" To which we would answer: "Habari," and they would answer: "Misuri," all with a friendly exuberance that touched the heart. I learned to say, "I sure wish I had a cold beer!" in Chagga (spoken in the homes of probably less than five hundred people), which was met with raised brows over big eyes, immediately followed by uproarious laughter: "How does *he* know *that?!*"

The horizon became a charcoal wall of volcanic sand. Like a tiny fleck of eggshell, Kibo Hut, at 16,620 feet, was barely discernable from a distance. The trail above the hut was apparent: a zigzag going up, two straight lines coming down.

I have spent nights in some rough places (a dirt-floored basement in Nepal comes to mind, its walls decorated with yak dung drying for fuel), but the conditions at Kibo are the most miserable I have ever encountered. The bare block building with a roof of corrugated metal is without heat or insulation. Outside, the only water is scooped from a fifty-five–gallon drum through a perpetual glaze of ice. At sea level in the tropics the hut would have been delightful, but to us, dog-tired and chilled to the bone, it offered little more than shelter from the wind. Most suffered from headaches or nausea, many were irritable, none could sleep: Oxygen deprivation was taking its toll.

At midnight the guides brought hot tea and cookies that nobody wanted. We stumbled out in the dark and started up. Two steps up, boots sinking into the loose gravel for one step down. It was a slow dance: thirty ponderous steps, then two full minutes of rest. Farther up it would be twenty steps; five near the top. It was helpful to take your thoughts away and enter a trancelike state of mind. Some would doze off while standing. The guides would chant, *"Pole, pole"* (Slowly, slowly), sometimes coming close to chuckle the mantra in your ear. After what seemed like a year, we came to Hans Meyer Cave, not a cavern, but a rock outcropping over a concave area, just large enough for five or six to lie close together in the dirt. No one wanted to get up. One did not move but declared that he was going down.

Then two more stumbled away. Soon after, another said he was going blind and turned around. The guides would tease, beg, and admonish, to encourage us to move ahead. Covered in high-tech, down-filled, extreme weather clothing, I was colder than I had ever been and prayed for the sun. A red line appeared, as thin as the first blood from a razor cut, curving ever so slightly across the horizon, hinting at the shape of the planet. It slowly became an orange stripe, then a band of yellow. Finally the sun caressed us like a warm glove. Clouds were at our feet. A few said they could go no farther. The guides pointed up to a field of boulders against a clear blue sky, "It's right *there!*"

We had climbed for eight hours since leaving Kibo when we attained the crater rim at Gillman's Point (18,700 feet). We had conquered the mountain. A few loose plaques in various languages were strewn around. Faded banners hung from metal staffs. Wedged into the rocks was an aluminum-bound, wooden box containing a pencil on a chain and a book of signatures. I wondered how often the guides replaced them and where they were stored. Some wanted photos. Most just lay down in the dirt and snow. Far across the crater was a fluted wall of ice cliffs hundreds of feet high. On other ascents some have traversed the rim to the true summit at 19,340 feet, but it is academic. Usually fatigue and concern about afternoon storms discourage the extra hike.

Down, down, down. Fast down. Warm down. Sliding and falling into the sand on weak legs down. Kibo far below down. We stopped at the hut to sleep for an hour, heat now passing through the thin metal covering. Then arising to go farther down. Out across The Saddle's hard surface. The pace quickening with the increasing oxygen. Passing Horombo, where a caretaker was selling warm beers, some stopped at the outhouse. By dusk we were at Mandara. The next morning was a two-hour walk to the park gate. At the hotel: Hot baths! Clean clothes! One climber's wife owned a gourmet shop; she had sent a large smoked salmon filet. Opening the foil we fell on it like wolves. We assembled on the lawn. The guides dressed up for the ceremony. They chanted songs in their language. One was just, "Kilimanjaro, Kilimanjaro..." to the clapping of their hands. Certificates were awarded. Some tears and sobs broke through.

Far away the crater cone was just a mound of black and white.

One of the hotel guests said it looked easy.

Cool Joe and the Animals

All rise up early hoping to see a kill.
The next day they hope not to see one.

El Condor

THE SIXTEEN HAD taken advantage of my offer of a climb of Mount Kilimanjaro and a camera safari across Northern Tanzania for a total cost of US$1,600 *including airfares.* Prior to entering the country we were required to complete Encashment Certificates listing the amounts and types of currency we were bringing in. Each exchange was to be noted and verified by the bank, hotel, or travel agency at the "official" rate, which was an arbitrary—and artificial—amount aimed at creating a false value for the Tanzanian shilling, and which had no relation to its actual worth when used to pay for goods and services.

We arrived in Arusha at midnight. Attempting to check in at our hotel we found our correspondence had been misread—1:00 PM not 1:00 AM—there was no room at the inn! We wandered down dark, dirt streets with snarling dogs rushing out to reflect our route. After the expedition members went to their rooms at an alternative hotel, the desk clerk asked if I would like to buy shillings at about half the state supported cost. She did not provide documentation for the transaction, and she called my room to ask, "Please do not mention the exchange to anyone!" After moving back to the New Arusha Hotel with its occasional corridor puddles from plumbing problems percolating through stained ceiling tiles, I bought more shillings at about four times less than their stated value, again without certification. On the climb of the mountain my down garments were so stuffed with large loaves of local cash that now and then a Velcro failure would allow several of the fist-sized bundles to roll out onto the trail. I explained the situation to a Dutch woman who said that if I contacted *Cool Joe* back in Arusha, he would solve all my problems.

The day we returned from climbing Mount Kilimanjaro was clear and pleasant. I decided to have a quart of Safari Larger in the hotel garden before going to my room. As soon as I sat down, two Tanzanians approached my table. One wore soft white Italian shoes, fitted cream-colored pants, a yellow silk shirt, and designer sunglasses of the type purchased by those whose tastes depend on the latest issue of GQ. No Manhattan club would have denied him entrance. He introduced himself as Cool Joe. His assistant wore a dark blue suit and tie in the tropical heat, and carried a stylish attaché case. He was the accountant.

Cool Joe noticed another man at a table within earshot and suggested that we move to a shaded area by a small creek in the most remote part of the grounds.

Prepared for complex negotiations, I began to explain each of our safari requirements in detail; each was waved away with the assurance that all would be provided at a competitive cost. He asked if we would like to change money. I said I would, but I would have to ask the other individuals. He named a rate of about five times the "official" value, and said those who wanted to do business should meet in my room (he already knew the number) in one hour, with their passports, Encashment Certificates, and currency.

When Cool Joe and his accountant came into my room they bolted the door, closed the blinds, and took the phone off the hook.

I explained that I had to change money at the street rate, but the others were free to do what they wished, and that I was not responsible for any problems that might occur. All except Charlotte, a CPA who objected on the grounds of illegality, decided to participate. The Africans assured us they would return in forty-five minutes as they left with our passports and most of our money.

An hour later my traveling companions began to question me as to what I had got them into. After an hour and a half I began to think about what recource we had.

A few minutes later there was a soft knock at the door. The two men came in carrying four huge grocery bags, each filled with bundles of shillings, each too large to grip in one hand. Some took photos of the great pyramid of cash that had been dumped onto the bed. Our certificates had been stamped, signed and sealed verifying the exchange of our foreign currency at the legal rate, including my previous transactions.

The next morning Cool Joe, his brother, and his uncle helped load our bags into the spacious van (which usually had to be push-started). We rolled away in the custody of Bill, our driver, who looked like Harry Belafonte.

More than fifty years before, Denys Finch Hatton, Isak Dinesen, Baron Delamere, and Bror Blixen, true adventurers, bold, strong risk takers, were drawn to Nairobi, Kenya, as expatriates. Their unconventional personal lives were minor manifestations of their independence. They chose the country because it was a British colony; however, their safaris took them south into German Tanganyika (Tanzania), then, as now, home to the world's biggest population of large wild animals. African nations have neglected to protect their wildlife. Internal corruption, foreign exploitation, and human overpopulation have all been factors. We have seen an increase in the number of animals, including the rarest species, in Tanzania. The cost, in the lives of park rangers as well as actual funds allocated, has been appreciable. One can only hope that such diligence will eventually reap returns.

Leaving Arusha, we came upon more and more Maasai. Isolation has helped their vivid culture remain intact. The men carry spears, wear tunics, and have their hair braided and colored with ocher mud. The women are adorned with beads and metal jewelry. All are tall and have a regal bearing. Every aspect of their lives sets them apart.

We crossed the Serengeti Plain to our farthest destination: Lake Ndutu tented camp. Late at night, while lying on our cots, we could hear the roar of a nearby lion, so deep and loud that it reverberated in our bones. It was an incomparable experience. At breakfast in the open dining room, colorful small birds flitted in to peck specks of egg and toast from the plates.

Having made prior arrangements with Mary Leakey, we were welcomed to the important archeological excavations at Olduvai Gorge. At the entrance someone took a classic photo of adolescent Karl wearing a Rolling Stones T-shirt with his arm around a Maasai warrior. Exploring the exposed strata, each layer recording millions of years, we were allowed to *pick up* and *keep* potshards and spear points fashioned by the earliest humans.

Recrossing the plain we stopped to buy sugar cane, cashew nuts, and sweet, plump fingerling bananas. While checking in at the National Park gate we heard screams from the woman who chose to wait in the van. Tearing the door open, Karl found a large male baboon holding a banana stalk and baring his needle-like canines. Reflexively Karl picked up a cane stalk and approached the animal that, with its powerful upper body and opposing thumbs, took the weapon away and eased in to counterattack.

After photographing some of the abundant elephants and giraffes that live in the park, we drove up to our lodge on the rim of the escarpment overlooking the Great Rift Valley to spend the late afternoon around the pool.

We slowly drove up the outer slopes of the great inactive volcano, Ngorongoro. At the highest point there was a break in the foliage. We stopped and were astounded: Thousands of feet below the crater floor was a grassy plain, ten miles in diameter. Tiny when viewed from above were vast herds of wildebeest, zebra, and cape buffalo. Even smaller were families of elephants. While having the highest concentrations of large animals in the world, this Eden was also the only habitat of the black-maned lion.

At the lookout, we were relieved that the second van had finally arrived. As it pulled to a halt beside us, Jeannie stepped from it, her smile bracketed by dimples; the girl-next-door with eyes that said her parents were not at home. At a glance you knew that she could not endure physical challenge, discomfort, or fatigue.

And you would be dead wrong.

Jeannie had trekked the Inca Trail with us. She was one of few who had chosen to breach a pass choked with nine-feet snowdrifts on the Milford Track in New Zealand, and she had reached the summit of Mount Kilimanjaro, the highest peak in Africa. She was the hostess of *P.M. Magazine, San Diego* and CBS had sent a film crew for her production of our camera safari. She would later become a star of the soap opera *Guiding Light.*

After a night at the lodge, we engaged guides and drivers for two Land Rovers to descend into the crater where we would set up tents and camp. I signed a paper handwritten in Swahili that I did not understand, but was told would save me US$150. I learned later that I had waived the requirement for an armed soldier to guard our camp. We slept each night with only a wisp of nylon between us and the wild animals prowling around our perimeter.

A loud, mischievous imitation of a snarling beast woke us up. The rear door of a vehicle opened and slammed shut as an actor friend of Jeannie's barricaded himself inside one of the Land Rovers until morning.

Jeannie's film crew set up reel-to-reel cameras on tripods in the midst of our camp. The resulting episode they produced would be chosen as one of the year's best by the network and rerun over and over.

A beautiful hotel was perched on the crater rim. We would stay there every year that followed. Forbidden to ascend to the hotel after dark, we bribed an armed patrol of rangers who allowed us to drive up for drinks and to return in "an hour or so." Three hours later we rumbled back across the valley floor in our Land Rovers. Suddenly, we were surrounded by another patrol aiming their automatic weapons at us and ordered to dismount with our hands above our heads. The guard had changed while we were above. Rick, who fancied himself a soldier of fortune, asked under his breath if we should "dive for the ditches?" I told him, "Don't fucking move!" We explained the situation to the soldiers, passed cigarettes around, and were allowed to return to camp.

At the tourist hotel in Arusha the residents' bars were dull and the nonresidents' bars were filled with prostitutes. The few small clubs around town were often at the end of an alley, marked only by a bare light bulb suspended over a single entrance door. The interiors were dimly lit, if lit at all. In the blackness Bob Marley's voice beat the walls. We were closer to Trenchtown, Jamaica, than indicated on maps. We were absorbed into the press of bodies without question, as though we were born a few miles away.

The shops were filled with merchandise chaotically piled on every horizontal surface, yellowed photos taken a decade before, Maasai spears with long flat blades, face collars surrounded with ostrich feathers.

In contrast, the extravagant outlets along the highway were Indian-owned, with cafes and restaurants, pristine restrooms, and overflowing with flawless new crafts that may or may not have passed through the hands of an African artisan.

Just after dark we stood packed and ready under the hotel entrance. It was already a half hour later than Bill should have arrived with our airport transportation, and the next KLM departure was three days later. I overheard Rick say, "Why isn't Buz *upset?*" The last Bill sighting had been at 3:00 AM that morning. His drunkenness was underwritten by my traveling companions' generous gratuities. After another thirty minutes I walked down a dark street for a couple of blocks to find it completely deserted. Returning down another street I almost stumbled over five men shooting craps on the sidewalk. I asked if two of them had cars to drive us to our flight and no one answered. I named an exorbitant figure for their doing so, and soon we were aboard old American vehicles from which body parts hung loosely and clanged together as we rode. As time had become critical, I offered a few extra shillings to the driver who arrived first at the terminal. The unlit, flat, straight, two-lane road to Kilimanjaro International Airport became a racetrack. Our Dodge Polaris shook and shuddered as though it were about to self-destruct. The other car honked and blinked its lights as it came alongside. One of its passengers screamed, "Tell them to slow down!"

At passport control it was called to my attention that my entrance stamp lacked a signature, and that I must have entered the country illegally. My choices were to appear in court the next day or pay a fine then and there and be allowed to board the waiting aircraft. I said that I would stay and that I could be contacted at the home of Ole Saibul, the conservator of Ngorongoro National Park and author of the wonderful *Herd and Spear*, about the Maasai. (I had met Mr. Saibul briefly, but he would not have remembered me.) The immigration clerk decided he could make an exception. His colleagues made fun of him.

Men and women were searched at separate kiosks. Each item of clothing and the entire contents of each carry-on parcel were examined slowly and deliberately while the examiner asked if you were taking out shillings. If you were, they wanted to know what you intended to do with them, along with a reminder that they were of no value outside the country. As soon as you agreed to hand over the shillings, everything else was handed back and you were allowed to board the airplane.

The customs officials were completely indifferent to the zebra hide (with certification of its death by natural causes) that one of us was taking out of the country. However, there was a squad of exceptionally large soldiers, clad in camouflage, combat boots and maroon berets, with only one concern—our Encashment Certificates. They read the certificates, held them up to the light, rubbed their thumbs across the signatures, and passed them around. We exhaled as they were handed back.

∼∼∼

Joe had proved to be *cool* indeed!

RETRIBUTION

So what do you do when he comes home
with the smell of another woman on him?
...you say, "PACK YOUR BAGS!"

Bette Midler

T ESSA HAS WOMEN friends that have been loyal for as long
as I have known her, and yet, I think she is more deeply
appreciated by men.

We met at Park Plaza Gardens. I was initially attracted by her
wit, then her intelligence (she was once the longest running contes-
tant on the longest running television quiz show), and then her mischievous smile. Her sheer black blouse had patch pockets that were
just a nod to modesty. Gamine, petite, and with a confidence that
proclaimed no dare would go untaken, how could she be ignored?

We have been friends ever since. She shows up as unexpectedly
and as welcome as early morning rain. There have been occasional
romantic incidents, which she calls accidents, without blame or
regret. One morning she called the architectural office at which
I was a design consultant, inviting me to come over right away. I
explained that I had a client conference in an hour. "Leave now!"
was her response.

The response reminded me of an incident when we were
returning from a camera safari and Mount Kilimanjaro climb.

95

We were delayed for four nights at the Nairobi Intercontinental, guests of KLM *while a new jet engine was brought from Amsterdam to replace the malfunctioning one on our grounded plane. The first day we timidly wondered if we were limited to the buffet or could order a la carte. By the third day we were demanding, "Where's the lobster salad? It was on the menu yesterday!" We also decided to have drinks, whether they were complimentary or not. One of our group, the type who agonizes over things, insisted upon asking the front desk if he owed a bar bill. He was charged* US$54. *Nothing about paying bar bills was mentioned to the rest of us. Finally we were notified that an airport bus was on the way to collect us. We passed from the Resident's Bar, where prostitutes were prohibited, through the Non-Resident's Bar, where there were at least a dozen such women clad in expensive dresses, bright against skin as matte black as unoiled ebony, with heavily made-up eyes and hair styled high in fashions as fantastic, complex, and bizarre as you could imagine. They were caricatures of sexuality, and any contact beyond the most casual was, literally, suicidal. However, they were interesting to observe and amusing to talk with, accomplished as they were in the ancient art of beguile-and-bargain. Care had to be taken to avoid diminishing what dignity they managed to maintain. As I passed her table, one of these women took my hand and murmured, "Take me to your room." I explained I had to catch a flight in thirty minutes. "Daddy, that's all it's going to take!" was the reply.*

Tessa's third husband opened a small wine shop serving sandwiches that evolved into a larger establishment with a good chef. It was a popular place, except on "music nights," when it was too loud to converse. One evening the husband catered a large party, during which my favorite (a better term than the juvenile "girlfriend" or the clinical "significant other") abandoned me after I talked to another woman. Late in the evening someone gave me a ride home, and after enough reconciliation,

I was allowed in to sleep. At 4:00 AM the phone rang. My favorite seemed shocked as she listened to the voice of her hysterical friend telling of escaping from the wine shop with her bare feet bloodied by broken glass. Yet not a word of what was said on the call was divulged to me at the time. It was not until months later that gossips told me as much as they knew and made up the rest.

Tessa had become concerned when it got late and her wine merchant husband had not come home. She stopped by the party host's house to find it deserted. So she went to the wine shop, and staring through the glass could barely see a naked couple rolling on the floor. She left in her Toyota with the lacrosse sticker emblazoned on it and returned in her husband's cream-colored Mercedes Benz convertible. Backing across the street, she gunned the engine until it roared, and then raced across four trafficless lanes. The sports car almost left the pavement at the crown of the road before crashing into the plate glass storefront more violently than anything seen in an over-budgeted, under-plotted action film. The police station was just blocks away, but no officer was summoned, nor did any appear. By morning, plywood sheets replaced the plate glass windows. (Fortunately, she missed the pipe columns; otherwise, the roof would have collapsed.) By nightfall, the windows had been reglazed and the low wall rebuilt.

Months later Tessa confided that after crashing the Mercedes into the front of the building, she had walked in through still falling shards of glass to push over wine racks ("I knew which were the most expensive") and chase her foolish spouse, beating him with a magnum of champagne, while the unknown "other woman" sat on the floor of the ladies' room listening to screams, her feet braced against the door.

The few who knew the mystery woman's name were, surprisingly, kind enough not to make it public, until a year later, when my by then not-so-favorite was talking with both her and Tessa at a social event. Another woman came over to exclaim, "It's wonderful to see you two as friends after that terrible thing happened!"

~~~

I have related this tale, with the help of mimicry, to Rwandan women by firelight, and to the interchangeable blondes of Helsinki at The Tractor Bar. It is invariably met with delirious laughter far beyond what the apparent humor deserves.

What sorrows have we men visited on the universal sisterhood that they would take such extreme delight in an act of harsh retribution?

A Tribute

> *The good shine from far away,*
> *Like the Himalaya mountains...*
>
> The Dhammapada

T HE SAND OF the isolated, endless beach has a foamy, frothy consistency that yields it cool underfoot on even the hottest days (a phenomenon that perhaps geologists can explain) and is lapped by white tongues of water so clear that when standing nipple-deep you can see your toenails. We sit by the *palapas* and sip our *café de olla* ("coffee of the pot," with a hint of cinnamon) and stare at the lightening sky.

The one wearing a *Members Only* windbreaker and a week's stubble is fifty-five years old and recently divorced. He says this is his first real vacation. He and his wife had taken a yearly business vacation at an all-inclusive resort to play golf each day, bridge each evening, and discuss business policies in between.

The other has a pipe clenched between teeth that form a mischievous grin as we wait to watch Guadalupe, the manager, walk naked to the surf and resent her boyfriend, Manolo, for the night they spent together.

The thatched huts that cost $5.00 per night later became a Buddhist retreat marketed out of Mill Valley, California, then a lesbian enclave with guests taking vows of silence, and are now available at $300.00 per night, with gatekeepers selling brochures designed and printed in New York City.

Six years later the grinning one called asking if I remembered him, and would I give advice on how to go back to the location with his teenage daughter. (Even now the very best of places are not all on the Internet and we sell their dwindling secrets to groups of those we esteem). It was *not* a place for teenage daughters. It was a place to heal after a disheartening divorce. It was a place to seduce your *novia.* It was a place to meditate alone on a New Year's morning. It was a place to live with your love on $3.00 worth of salsa, cheese, and bread per day. Even the best of teenage daughters voice complaints about sand in their sheets and having to squat in the sea oats behind the dunes.

Later, he traveled with us to watch humpbacked whales play on Samana Bay in the Dominican Republic and dance in the old hippie's bar until dawn. In an open boat on the rolling sea (the rest biliously clinging with white knuckles to the gunwales), he puffed his pipe and told stories of the Marine Corps as though we were in the lounge of a gentlemen's club.

He had also ridden rough economic high seas, once telling his wife and children that the house and car were lost. (A young banker granted two weeks more, and saved them.) He sold ice cream from a *Good Humor* truck.

He contracted the adventure virus, causing him to join us to scale the Devil's Staircase in Bolivia, drive sled dogs across frozen lakes in Finland, swim with sharks in the Galapagos Islands, and face without blinking the high-heeled kicks of tango dancers in Argentina.

As oblivious to pain as to danger, a doctor in the Andes had to persuade him that urine the color of Guinness was *not* an innocuous symptom.

A great measure of financial success has come to him that only the most mean-spirited would begrudge. It has come for two reasons: his loyalty and his honesty.

He knows wealth is only a patina on the surface of his true success: that admiration which has always existed in the hearts of his daughters, step-daughters, friend's wives, girlfriends, and that very little girl who calls him "Papa."

And in the regard of those who call him "Friend."

A Taste Of Something Stronger

Listen, I will be honest with you,
I do not offer the old smooth prizes,
but offer rough new prizes.

Song of the Open Road
Walt Whitman

O NE SUNDAY AFTERNOON *an architect friend and his*
wife introduced me to a man who had just returned
from Peru. This man's smooth manner became agitated
as he described hiking the switchbacks from the river up to the
magnificent ruins of Machu Picchu, "The Lost City of the Incas."
While there he had also heard of an ancient Inca trail through
the Andes to the remote stone metropolis.

Daniel claimed his middle name was Boone. He had a mischievous manner and the engaging conversational ability of a born salesperson. Only when he shifted, without warning, to an evangelical mode, did he become boring. Without hesitation Daniel agreed to trek the Inca Trail with me and take his thirteen-year-old son, Drew, along. The boy was intelligent and sensitive, and had already distinguished himself as a talented golfer. Surprisingly, his mother, a tall, willowy beauty, consented to his joining what, even to me, seemed a rather foolhardy venture.

Without any reliable knowledge of what lay ahead, we boarded the old steam train and chugged out of Cuzco, Peru, on narrow gauge tracks. The only other passengers intending to attempt the challenge were two German mountain climbers. They were going to trek in the direction opposite from the one advised. The climbers copied their hand-drawn map on a paper bag for us.

When the conductor stopped the train at kilometer 88, we were the only ones to disembark. The train cars disappeared into a rough tunnel cut into high cliffs. We silently stared at a bridge of handmade rope swinging high above a chocolate-milk river churning over boulders the size of buses. At the far end, a small path continued away. I took a deep breath of the cool, clean air and realized that being there was just a taste of something stronger than the usual. From then on, weaker brews would never be acceptable.

We walked switchbacks up a sheer wall covered with bromeliads to a notch that opened to a long valley. All day we followed a river upstream. It became more narrow and rapid as the mountains on the other side came closer. As our altitude increased, the percentage of oxygen in the ambient air fell, causing our steps to be slower and our packs to seem heavier. This linked pattern of topography and fatigue was to be repeated over and over. Fog wetted us as the afternoon wore on. I had erroneously assumed that summer in Peru would be the best time to explore. Alas, heavy clouds hid some of the most dramatic white peaks in our hemisphere. On later visits, during clear, dry winters, the great spectacles would be revealed.

When we felt we could go no farther, we walked into a circle of a few thatch-roofed stone huts at the confluence with another stream. I met Paulino Herrera, the Headman of Wayabamba, who became my friend and welcomed us each subsequent year. I have seen his son, Juan, grow to manhood and continue the family. A barefooted little girl was playing in the mud. I am the godfather of her daughter, an adult whom I see each time I return.

The schoolhouse had one dirt-floored room, with no door or windows in the openings. Chairs were piled in the least exposed corner. Although the villagers spoke only Quechua, we understood that we were welcome to camp in their midst. We were asked to refrain from shitting in the cornfields. At dawn the entire village came out to say goodbye and direct us onto the right path.

We trekked through tropical cloudforests, across open meadows and up muddy climbs, occasionally fording calf-deep creeks, always toward a U-shaped gap that never seemed any closer. I came to know it well as the First Pass. Once over the pass, we dropped down quickly and lost the trail in a maze of rotting vegetation through which we often sank to our waists. To our relief we finally came upon the trail. When it forked there was no indication of which was the way to the ruins. The valley was uninhabited. We called it the "Valley of the Moon" for its heavy mists and twisted trees encrusted with lichen and dripping with moss. Doubting that we should descend in order to climb back up, we chose the higher route. We were wrong. Eventually there was nothing left to follow. We were in a steep field of boulders with no idea how to proceed. It was a slow, difficult climb to a higher pass that was not *the* Second Pass on the Inca Trail to Machu Picchu. As we stumbled down, total darkness enveloped us.

Hours later we thought we saw a light and started yelling into the void. An old Quechua woman suddenly appeared in front of us. She turned around and we followed. In a corner of her mud-floored hut, a log of wood was burning. She crumbed pieces from a brick of coarse, sugary chocolate into a battered pot of water. We passed around a rough clay cup filled with the delicious liquid. She indicated that Drew could sleep in the same room with her and the flame, but that we adult males would have to stay in the other room. It was empty, except for the drying carcass of a small animal.

The next day she put us on the proper route and for two days we passed above buttresses and by walls of stone crafted by ancient masters of masonry. The massive boulders were locked together by mortarless joints too tight to admit a knife blade.

Along the way Dan declared, "Buz, you buzz*ard,* here your nickname should be 'El Condor'," and it stuck. Considered an affectation by my "stateside" friends, many in South America know me only by that *apodo.*

The fourth night we saw lights from what seemed to be a conventional building far below us. We wound down a narrow trail until a high wooden gate barred our way to the small hotel. One jamb of the gate was implanted into the vertical hillside; the other hung over a sheer drop hundreds of feet deep. The chain on the gate was padlocked. We pounded and shouted until someone answered that the gatekeeper had left for the night. Drew went first, working his way around the outside edge of the barrier. Dan tried next, but his arms were unable to hold his bulk. I saw his hands slip, but could do nothing as he slapped at the wood, screamed, and fell. After he crashed through the treetops, all was silent.

Finally, Dan's weak voice called up that he was hurt, but would try to climb up. Branches had stopped his fall. I was hugging his sobbing son when he finally scrambled up to meet us. The public areas of the hotel on the other side of the gate were deserted, but someone took Dan and Drew to a resident doctor, while I woke the only waiter and asked for a drink. He grudgingly gave me a used paper cup filled with *pisco.* It was my first taste of the clear, strong Andean brandy, and it warmed me to my chilled fingertips. Dan returned with his chest taped. Part of his pectorals had been torn from his breastbone.

The doctor invited us to spend the night. Wet, cold, tired, and hungry, I envisioned us sipping drinks in easy chairs before a large fireplace while the doctor's wife prepared a feast. In reality, he lived in a small, unheated room at the end of the Quonset hut that served as his laboratory. A couple traveling together, he from Martinique, she from Sweden, had also been asked to stay. We all had some extra packets of powdered freeze-dried dinners, one each of which, reconstituted in boiling water, had been our sole daily sustenance. We were elated at being indoors for the night and having plenty to eat.

In the room were three narrow beds. The men removed only their boots, but the woman took off everything she wore. Her pale skin glowed in the light from the cans of burning Sterno. The couple slipped beneath the blanket of one bed and Dan and Drew stretched out in the second. Just as I reflected on the luxury of having a bed to myself, our host asked me to move over. For hours I lay perfectly still, staring up at the curved corrugated ceiling, until a dreamless sleep enclosed me.

<div align="center">~~~</div>

So began a long association with Peru. In the following years we would train for ninety days prior to our departure for the country by climbing stairs with forty-pound packs, working our quadriceps at the gym and on weekly bicycle rides. Thirty days out I would stop drinking and the pounds would melt away. A few nights dissipation in Cuzco would negate the efforts. On the first of the trail's steep inclines I would regret the decision to return.

At Wayabamba the locals came to expect us, once greeting me with a blackened iron kettle of *chicha,* a frothy beer homemade from yucca. I palmed water purification pills into the liquid. The iodine ingredient immediately turned the starch purple, eliciting an "Ahaa..." from the villagers.

Paulino asked us to cure eight-year-old Juan's abscessed tooth. Loath to disillusion him, we decided on extraction. Juan's father held his shoulders and sweat ran down the boy's face as we tried the Swiss Army knife tools in vain. Paulino would not agree to our suggestion of administering pisco, and instead stuffed a wad of coca leaves into the healthy side of his son's mouth. After endless attempts with dental floss looped around the discolored tooth, we finally yanked it free. Two years later Juan had another dental problem, and we took up a small collection sufficient to cover train fares to Cuzco and dentist's fees.

Whiling away the afternoon and resting in the yard among the huts, one young trekker sailed a stone at a foraging chicken. To his surprise the stone hit the target and the hen fell down in a fit of flapping wings, grasping claws, and pathetic clucks. Everyone not working the fields rushed out. One woman cradled the fowl in her arms as tears ran down her face. The grief was not for a barnyard pet, but for a reduction in their limited food sources. Appalled at what had happened, we offered the usual North American solution—money. The woman was placated and everyone seemed relieved. A short while later the hen came limping out with a splint on its left drumstick that would have done an orthopedist proud.

Views of mammoth chalk-white glaciers became our visual reward each time we crossed the high passes.

Forgetting that at high altitude water boils at a lower temperature than required to render it antiseptic, a soccer coach and a man and his wife, both attorneys, made coca tea. The infusion does not alter consciousness, but effectively opens a larger volume of the bronchial system to oxygen. It did not, however, kill the bacteria in the water. After drinking the tea the two men stricken with "Atahualpa's Revenge" could walk, but the wife had to be helped along. When a Quechua couple came around the cliffs, a villager accompanying us translated the lawyer's offer to buy their horse at any price. The man refused, stating simply, "It is *my* horse!" (I received a similar response years later in Mexico when I tried to purchase a large drinking gourd in a remote area.) It is difficult for us, who are taught that money is everything, to understand that some things are not for sale.

On the other hand, some things are.

A few times we traversed earth-slides caused by dynamiting for the construction of a hotel within a day's hike of Machu Picchu. The building process was so slow that the lodging became old and dilapidated before completion. It did, however, provide hoses for washing ourselves down, toilets that sometimes flushed, and crowded floor space in front of a fireplace. We ate all the food and drank everything in sight, including the contents of some blue medicine bottles with handwritten labels.

Unbeknown to us, the manager sent his pregnant wife down the serpentine stone trail on horseback in the dark to the ruins. She returned with two cases of beer. We would have objected to her making the dangerous trip, but we probably would not have objected enough.

It was a white-knuckle bus ride from Machu Picchu along sheer drop-offs down to Aguas Calientes by the river, where the only buildings were the train station and the "tourist hotel," which promised warmth, shelter, and sustenance. It was exciting to enter the large space that served as a bar, restaurant, and reception room. At this social and cultural center for the entire region, the patrons were backpackers, archaeologists, Quechuas, a few daring tourists, and three men with dark skins sporting large hoop earrings and hair to their waists. I told our group to pile their packs in the corner and take seats around them. This all seems unduly melodramatic now that the town boasts expensive resort hotels, dozens of restaurants, and a gauntlet of craft stalls through which thousands of tourists weave their way. We ordered liter bottles of Cusqueña beer, the pride of the nation. (Once, while passing through endless fields of barley, I commented that the grain must feed a large segment of the population. I was told that it all went to the brewery in Cuzco.) My negotiations yielded one room with ten single bunks at thirty-five U.S. cents each for the sixteen of us. The concrete floor stunk of urine, but the sheets, printed with Disney characters, were fresh and clean. When the women went to the adjacent restrooms, two of us would stand outside the doorless opening holding our knives. Again, this might have been unnecessary, but it seemed prudent at the time. Those in upper outside bunks on the street side could have reached through paneless clerestory windows and touched the heads of passersby (had they wanted to). Late at night there were some screams from the street that were horrific.

At dawn, my first vista through a cracked and clouded window was of two pigs fucking by the railroad tracks: Good Morning, Aguas Calientes.

∼∼∼

Beyond the famous ruins, the train tracks begin a gentle constant descent into the upper reaches of the Amazon Basin. Debbie, my friend and latter-day business partner, accompanied me to the town of Quillabamba, the first train destination in the "eyebrow of the jungle." We had come to know Giovanni, who was the chef and owner of a different restaurant each time we returned. He was known for his wife, who looked like an aging Cher, and for his ability to supply a white powder at short notice. It is fortunate that the drug has never attracted me. *Gratifying simpler, more basic appetites is all my meager resources can afford.*

Quillabamba was anticlimactic after the dramatic train trip from which, deep in the jungle, the white peak of Salcantay could be seen rising miles behind. I remember coffee that tasted like chocolate, chocolate that tasted like coffee, and the same sense of isolation that draws us back to islands such as Santorini and Rapa Nui.

Casual contacts had advised us to "beware of the fruit ladies." We supposed they were concerned about the Quechua women who dominated each coach by pushing passengers against the windows with flaring layers of dirty crinolines and bulging sacks of produce. At 4:00 AM, native women wrestling huge bags of tropical produce dominated the station platform

for our return trip. As they boarded the train, a military officer inserted a thin chrome probe into a sampling of melons,
papayas, and cantaloupes to extract a narrow spoonful of the
contraband within. A record was kept, not to establish guilt,
not to be used as evidence, but to quantify the *mordida* (bribe)
to be paid on the return trip after sales had been made.

Hiram Bingham, Yale professor and eventual governor of
Connecticut, writes eloquently in *The Lost City of the Incas* of "the
witchery of the jungle" below peaks running along the mighty
Urubamba River, but his words are as weak as water compared to
the astonishing experience of the train ride through the Sacred
Valley returning from the ruins of Machu Picchu. The river itself,
surfing high over gigantic boulders, defies the written word.
There are some tough individuals among the whitewater captains of Peru, but none even considers braving such rapids. There
is a stopover at El Alburge in Ollantaytambo that one should
not miss. Family and friends of the owner staff the small hotel
by the train tracks. The Internet can supply archeological facts
and items of interest to the casual tourist at the nearby World
Heritage site. Instead, I write of the delights of a primitive sauna
with the pungent aroma from eucalyptus leaves on hot stones,
the icy hose water over naked bodies in the dark, and of the night
I, half drunk, generously gave insider travel tips to a mild-mannered North American. At breakfast, to the delight of all, I was
told the man was Peter Frost, expatriate author of some of the
best guidebooks about Peru ever published in English.

The train would come over the crest of a hill as we neared
Cuzco. At sunset the interior lights would dim and there was
silence. From the speaker came the throb of a drum, then the
pulse of a guitar, overridden by the high, haunting melody
on a pan flute—"El Condor Pasa," the stirring anthem of the
Inca Empire. Only the dull, the callous, the insensitive are not
touched. At the station we strapped our packs in front of us and
held our knives in our fists as we pushed through the crowd.

For over thirty years I guided treks of the Inca Trail, until the route became an endless line of tourists, and the ruins a congestion of sightseers. We still visit the mammoth citadel of stone, but our hikes now are through remote villages known to few: Silent. Serene. Spectacular.

∿∿∿

Even if there was no hot water, we basked in hotel showers then descended to Cuzco's Plaza de Armas, "hungry, horny, and heinous" as my New Mexican friend described those coming back from the Molybdenum mines. First to *La Yunta* ("The Yoke"), named for two partners, to savor cream soups strong with flavors of giant vegetables from the fertile valleys, pizzas coated with garlic, and whipped drinks of fresh juice laced with pisco. As we ate and drank, small boys would chant and play for tips. Tourists often remark on the cuteness of their rosy cheeks. The inflammation is caused by a low-grade infection on their chronically chapped faces. On to *Quehatachuay,* a cavernous, darkened upstairs room with continuous live music, where your count of aguardiente consumed was accepted on the honor system and where tourists were a rarity. Then to places to dance such as *Kamikaze,* where they would project videos of our adventures on large screens to the over-amplified music of Dire Straits or R.E.M. One of our trekkers danced so violently that her blistered feet bled and she had to be carried to her room. If you had a *carina* you took her to *Muki,* where Peruvian couples searched for privacy in manmade biomorphic caves away from the crowded homes of their extended families. Other nights we would go to *El Truco,* which featured continuous indigenous music and an extensive menu of Andean fare. On each table stood a small flag designating its occupants' nationality. Here camaraderie took priority over political differences as the master of ceremonies promoted applause when introducing each country. The exception was a table seating a dozen Chilean officers in olive-brown uniforms and their wives in prom dresses from another era. Their kind had tortured their own countrymen and women, throwing some from airplanes high over the Pacific. There was a full minute or more of silence while all present stared at them with repugnance, before the speaker moved on.

On one such Farewell Dinner night my friend, Lucho, was to escort young Libby to the festivities. Her father, Dr. Stilton, had brought her with us in an effort to mend the damage done by a recent divorce aggravated by a nurse's sexual harassment suit. He was far more protective than her age and independent travel experience required. Martha Mahoney and Jim Easterling had agreed to be chaperones, but at the last minute they pled fatigue and I was pressed into service. The doctor asked that I make sure Libby was back in the hotel by midnight. Having my own romantic agenda, I resented the obligation. At the appointed time Libby asked that we wait in the lobby for a few minutes. She returned to say that her father had agreed to her and Lucho staying out later. At 3:00 AM my room telephone rang; it was the doctor demanding to know his daughter's whereabouts. I explained and tried to go back to sleep. Because of the Spanish siege mentality (and the real threat posed by a countryside in the throes of rebellion) public buildings locked their massive doors by midevening. My room had a balcony just above the entrance. At dawn I heard the couple's voices and the slam of the antique knocker echo along the empty street. At the airport the doctor's eyes had dark circles under them, and the daughter's were tear-reddened. They both apologized.

We had breakfast on the mezzanine awaiting our flight departure for Lima. A deep roar increased until it seemed that a plane was about to come through the terminal walls. The table shook. The floor shook. The waiter threw his tray aside and ran. Jim looked at me and said, "Earthquake!" And then came the sound of breaking glass. As we started down, the open stairs began to undulate. Some jumped safely from the landing.

In the space below Quechuas pushed against the tall concrete columns. There were at least ten pairs of plate glass exit doors. All were chained and padlocked except one. We stood outside in groups watching the building and hugging and sobbing. We thought that all of us were safely outside. But we had overlooked a hairdresser from Westerville, Ohio, whom we had dubbed "Hollywood." He liked to wear black leather from wrist to ankle and had a penchant for ingesting mind-altering substances. As the tremors subsided, he stepped out from amid the clouds of plaster dust, looked around, smiled and said, "Wow!"

My daughter left her room, unaware there had been an earthquake. She had resisted my insistence that she accompany her group to the airport to catch their flights. Half asleep, she thought the cataclysmic roar was me banging on her door, angry at her irresponsibility.

~~~

The horseback trips gave us the range to explore remote, sparsely inhabited regions. Riding for days along the rims of gorges or across high plains, breaking only for lunch or a dip in a thermal spring, we would come to a cluster of huts. At one tiny village, the residents came out in festive dress. Our guides explained that no other outsiders had been there since we came through five years before.

At one stop my horse went down as though shot. To the delight of all, I was left standing with a leg on each side of the fatigued Andean pony.

Following Barry, I was entertained by watching him slowly bounce farther to one side of the saddle until, after a few miles, he would fall to the ground.

Matt, usually stoned, would try to mount from the wrong side while the horse would whirl, wide-eyed, in circles. To my suggestion, he yelled, "I don't need any equestrian tips from you!"

Each night, camped a short way from us, the wranglers could be heard laughing uproariously. Someone asked, "What do you suppose they find so funny?"

Lucho reported that, if we let them know in advance, the village at which we would stay would cook a sheep for us in the traditional manner. I informed the group, and all agreed to pay the US$2.00. Along the way some asked if one animal would be enough; could they have chicken also? And would they prepare some vegetables as side dishes? *Forgive them, Father, for they know not where they are.* I passed Lucho's answer that a second sheep could be purchased. As we dismounted, I was told that the tiny village could only afford to give up one sheep for the barbeque. I announced the news, adding that this was not my deal anyway. Joe spoke out: "It was your deal when it was a two-goat deal!" Even now, when she thinks I am shirking responsibility, Debbie says, "It was your deal when it was a two-goat deal!"

A butchered carcass hung from a tree in the midst of the few dwellings. The fire pit was covered with flat stones that made cracking noises as the heat increased from the embers below. Pieces of meat were heaped directly onto the searing stones. Fiber sacking was placed on the mound, then a pile of freshly cut grass. Dirt was shoveled on top and, as smoke seeped up, the mound was wrapped in more sacking. The entire procedure took only minutes and was as choreographed as a Broadway musical. Lucho again suggested I take up a collection for beer from a nearby town, the first to be seen in days. He returned to say he had purchased seven bottles, all that was available. Fortuitously, the beer bottles held two liters each, and we happily drank the warm Cusqueña. Yellow-meated Peruvian potatoes (one of the approximately one hundred and fifty varieties available in the country) were to accompany the feast. After cooking, they were placed in a large bag. As we watched, the communal pig ran by, took the sack in its teeth and trotted away, cooked tubers rolling in its wake. In exactly the predicted three-quarters of an hour, the main course was ready. The savory flavors piqued our appetites. We invited the village and there was plenty for all, with leftovers for breakfast.

Dave Roberts likes to quote, "Even a blind hog finds an acorn now and then." As we lay back satiated and content after our feast, Dave closed his eyes, pushed his nose into a snout, and made grunting noises.

≈≈≈

Awaiting the arrival of a second, non-trekking group, Bill and I shared a hotel room, which we decorated with wool tapestries and calla lilies. One night a young Aymara girl from the Lake Titicaca area invited herself in to raise funds to buy a Sony Walkman. As I patted the sheets saying, *"Aqui, aqui,"* Bill's insufficiently muffled laughter from the next bed disrupted the negotiations and she left. The desk clerk/bartender was a small boy with a self-deprecating manner and a squeaky voice. The owner was deducting the cost of a stolen pisco-sour blender from his meager earnings. We paid off the debt and gained the clerk's relentless fawning admiration. As we crossed the lobby in the morning he exclaimed, "Condor, the woman just left your room!" He was mistaken. Another guest must have underwritten the purchase of the Walkman.

Susan was equal to any occurrence, but her friend, Margaret, was emotionally delicate. An Argentine hustler and his German girlfriend invited themselves to our table at *La Trattoria*. When the couple got up without paying, I called them on it and the man threw some coins down and yelled foul curses before he and his girlfriend hurried out the door. A few days later we came upon him selling wire jewelry on the sidewalk of Avenida del Sol in Cuzco. Without hesitating, Bill bent his arm back as I choked his bandana around his neck. A crowd gathered while Bill demanded an apology. As he gurgled it out, I noticed two soldiers with automatic weapons watching the show, and was relieved when they shook our hands, saying that the cheap con man deserved such treatment. Margaret was visibly shaken.

Days later, while rafting the upper Urubamba, we passed the girlfriend soaping her naked body by the shore. Her new companion was obviously embarrassed. He wore the red-stripped pattern that bespeaks the Uros, a group that is inherently humble after years as subjugates of the Incas, slaves of the Conquistadors, and recently, beasts of burden for large tour companies, staggering up narrow trails with brutal double loads. The woman's guttural insults carried easily over the water.

At the time, seventy percent of Peru (although sparsely populated areas) was controlled by the Shining Path, a Marxist uprising independent of international influences begun by two professors at the University of Arequipa. There were few incidents in the large cities, except that on occasional mornings the citizens of Lima would venture out to find dead dogs hanging from lampposts. Cuzco, the repository of indigenous culture, was another matter. During a folkloric performance attended by four women in our group, the adjacent police station was bombed. The next day was *El Dia de la Madre* (Mother's Day), a surprisingly popular holiday in South America. Large, swarthy mustached men can be seen carrying boxes of decorated cakes. By nightfall they are drunk. Long parades pass by receiving stands filled with military officers. The festivities begin at dawn, not with a traditional 21-gun salute, but with the stuttering fire from a machine gun mounted in the center of the Plaza de Armas. Fire hoses on tracked vehicles are manned at each exit from the public squares. When I knocked on one elderly woman's door, a dark-circled eye appeared above the chain lock, then a timid voice inquired, "Are they bombing again?"

Bill decided to stay behind after the trek. Susan, Margaret, and I took too long over our railway station coffee and rushed to board the train as the engine was building up steam.

Hurrying on to the closest carriage, we were told our seats were in the next car back. We found our way there and settled in. As the train started to move away from the station an explosion shook our carriage as though it were a toy. Across the aisle a man yelled, "It's just an air line!" It's just an air line!" Screams came from the car we had moved through to find our seats. From the passageway I could see smoke, dust, and a hole the size of a bathtub ripped in the carriage roof. Soon blood-covered people were being carried past our windows. One man, fully conscious, cradled his iridescent intestines in his arms. Soldiers directed us back to the coffee shop where we were briefly questioned by plainclothesmen. Surprisingly, a United Press International stringer from St. Petersburg, Florida, called me at the hotel. He had not been able to obtain early information about the incident from his sources. A friend of Susan's father saw his article in a London daily and contacted him in Los Angeles. A small picture of Susan and Margaret illustrated a story in *Oiga,* a weekly Peruvian magazine. Headlines about "LA MOCHCHILA ROJA" (The Red Backpack) appeared in all the Peruvian newspapers. The explosive devise had been concealed in a pack and placed in the overhead rack. As there had been no previous attacks by the Shinning Path on tourists, some believed the government had precipitated the incident to increase the opposition to the rebels.

The *Autowagon* replaced the old train. Priced to isolate tourists, it had wraparound windows, a stewardess serving coffee and snacks, and a military officer in attendance.

The Uros still rode in boxcars.

After returning to Seattle, Margaret was in therapy for months.

∽∽∽

Ney was a charlatan, a "rice Christian" brought up by missionaries. His tiny black eyes gleamed with guile above a wraparound smile similar to that of some poisonous snakes.

We were going to take a large free-floating raft down seven hundred miles of the Huallaga, Marañón, and Amazon Rivers. Ney was in charge of every aspect of the journey, which only increased my concern.

Our first night was in Tarapoto, Peru, just above the top-ographic slope down to the jungle. The small mountain town seemed prosperous, with clean cobbled streets and cool dry air with oxygen in short supply. Ney brought a woman to dinner. Her pale skin and round face were not typical of the local people. A black braid hung to her waist. She spoke little, smiled often, and followed me to my room.

Among those on the trip was Jerry, a printer by trade, who was both tough and gentle, a rare and admirable combination. He and his brothers had "done a few things," such as being air-lifted into the Yukon and left with basic supplies to stay for months, panning just enough gold to make it worthwhile. His scarred face was always ready to smile.

Annette had lived with a famous poet in San Francisco, around whom the so-called Beat Generation was formed.

Jimmy owned a popular bar/restaurant in Winter Park, Florida. He was a Vietnam veteran who seldom spoke of the war, but when he did, it was without whining or bravado and his words had the "ring of truth," like a ship's brass bell. His friend, Von Eisman, was quiet, but always carried a holstered .357 Magnum.

Andy was a professional photographer. He raved about the tropical flowers, and was as flamboyant and overbearing as their colors. He had done some jail time on a minor narcotics charge. I think he might have enjoyed the experience.

A Hollywood attorney, whom I did not recruit, represented the estates of deceased celebrities, such as Marilyn Monroe, and the interests of living ones such as Sophia Loren and Carlo Ponti. His camera straps crossed a flowered shirt that hung over his belly. Shorts and dress shoes completed the ensemble. He thought he had all the answers and was willing to share them.

Our craft for the first two days of the trip was a platform with a single waist-high rail. Two oarsmen tied to the barrier each manned a long, broad-bladed sweep oar; such rafts have navigated the upper river system since before the conquest. Although the rapids were not high, one could sense the volume and velocity of the river. It moved as a single entity, like a massive milk chocolate serpent sliding between the banks. We hung on and laughed, and sometimes screamed.

Our first night on the river was spent tied up to the bank while we slept aboard. The next night we were the entertainment for a small remote village. Andy traded for a bizarre black bird with neck wattles, which accompanied him for the entire journey.

The next morning we were stunned by the sight of our new home: rough planks covering two layers of three-feet diameter submerged logs. Over half the planked area was a structure covered entirely by thatch, enclosing a dining area and three sleeping rooms with hammocks. Each space was defined by partial partitions. A ladder led to a platform built into the roof, just large enough for a hammock. A couple of hens roosted in the fronds. A small, enclosed latrine hung over the edge of the deck, next to the propane stove from which buckets hung—the galley. Lashed to the sides were two dugout canoes with small outboard engines, our only power. They were not used to move the craft. When we cast off we moved with the current's whim, sometimes straight downstream, sometimes in slow spins like dancers moving across a ballroom. The meandering alluvial avenue was lined with walls of trees that rose almost out of sight. For a couple of days there were no signs of human life.

Aside from Ney, the crew consisted of two boatmen, a cook, and four adolescent women to assist her, sweep and serve meals. The girls were a delight to watch. Shy around us, they chattered softly in a language only the cook understood. Each day they were clean and well dressed. Very late at night they would bathe and launder alongside the raft. A passenger tried to persuade them to smoke some pot he had purchased in Tarapoto. They looked to the cook for guidance. With a grin she dismissed the proposition as inconsequential, but spoke in awe of *ayahuasca,* the complex hallucinogen used by the most remote tribes of the region. A woman from the Ministry of Tourism was along to report on our voyage. While telling a story at dinner I accidentally bumped her hip, which threw her into a tirade. She was protective of the girls, which they found puzzling.

Meals were always a surprise. One night I was served a turtle's claw on a bed of white rice. Tabasco sauce was in demand. There was a menagerie of other animals aboard, Andy's vulture, chickens, and a tame *javelina,* a dwarf pig covered with long charcoal bristles over a body that was indistinct except for the snout. Its tiny hooves could be heard dancing around the deck at all times. The passengers adopted it as a pet, which prevented (or delayed) its execution. As the current became sluggish, we would go on excursions in one of the dugouts. Once, as we cast off, we heard a shout and looked back to see a machete come down on the night's main course.

A native family in a canoe pulled alongside to trade a string of fish, which were left uncleaned in the sun all day. When I came home I was beset by sporadic attacks of flatulence and diarrhea, which were diagnosed as giardia. The gastroenterologist blamed the fish.

Upstream in the clearer tributaries we would fish for piranhas with cane poles. On the edge of their flat hand-sized bodies were tiny eyes above a small mouth ringed with needle teeth. We were told that it was not dangerous to swim in their midst as they were scavengers that attacked only dead or dying carcasses. We reluctantly went over the side. Though not very agile in the water, when something touched my leg I performed an impressive leap into the boat. On the way back to the raft, Andy discovered a brilliant mass of flowers high above us and said he would "just *love* to have it." Von Eisman said, "I will get it for you." With that he drew his pistol and blew away the entire treetop. Red and green confetti slowly drifted down on us.

An open platform raft passed carrying only a pyramid of swollen burlap bags and two men holding automatic rifles. We followed the crew's example and acted as if they did not exist.

Twice we ran aground. All went overboard into neck-deep water and labored until we were free.

Shacks began to appear along the riverbank. We stopped to see one with a large jaguar hide nailed to the wall. Each dwelling had a power line and a bare bulb or two. A little farther inland oil companies had built camps.

At the first town we went ashore. Ney arranged a volley-ball match between the passengers and the local girls' team. He urged us to bet with him. When we lost, he claimed his winnings would be donated to the school. He liked to tell of his donations, probably as a result of his missionary upbringing.

The river became calm and too wide to see across. Boredom set in. Most of our time was spent in the hammocks, sleeping or reading.

Our odyssey ended at the isolated town of Iquitos. Situated there is a large community of wood structures connected by ladders and planks that, when the water is high, floats near the bank. When we arrived the rains had not come, so the homes were stuck on mudflats that stank of human waste.

On the way to the airport Ney claimed that he had donated the raft to a church and the pet pig to a local zoo.

There are things that are more enjoyable to tell about than to experience.

~~~

Chando, a Peruvian, was educated in California. He and a friend began, with one rubber raft, a company that was to become famous throughout Latin America. He is charismatic, athletic, and astute in business matters. The number of rubber rafts grew as other daring young men came to apprentice themselves, often living in communal quarters on Chando's property. Some of the young men's lives faltered over the temptations of accessible drugs, and their marriages sank from too many adoring tourist women hoping for thrills beyond the whitewater. Most overcame the adversities to become known almost as well as their mentor. The venture grew. Chando would obtain permission to explore rivers in protected areas. Cuzco investors underwrote the first descents, their reward coming when the pioneer's route was offered to the public. Our small company was fortunate to grow with them. Crossing Chile on the Bio-Bio before it was dammed (and damned), other whitewater groups would bob in the eddies, allowing Chando's team to enter each rapid first with his craft in the lead. Legends emerged, such as Fico, who would wrap a wet bandana around his head in lieu of a helmet and stand in the pitching raft, paddle held high, before they were quite beyond the last turbulence. Pepe, who was the subject of stories and sketches in an early Banana Republic catalogue. Mendel, married to the police chief's beautiful daughter. Mischievous Lucho, with an unerring antenna tuned to the next party or the nearest willing woman.

We worked our way from the comparatively gentle Upper Urubamba, through the Apurimac, the "Speaker of the Gods," to the mighty Tambopata and the "Trip From Hell."

Chando boarded our bus at the airport, introduced himself, and announced that we were on an expedition, not an excursion. Some snickered at the melodrama.

The next morning we were seated in the body of a bus mounted on the bed of a large trailer truck, crossing the *Altiplano.*

After thirteen hours, including a brief stop for a meal and the purchase of pisco, we stopped by a small village, unrolled our bags and slept beneath the truck until first light.

In a small town we were stopped by a military contingent of adolescents. We handed our passports to the ranking officer who was obviously drunk. One guide's document was Chilean, as his father was a diplomat. The officer claimed he was a spy. It took Chando thirty minutes to cajole him with jokes about the tourists "going to see the birds." *We were aware of a Swiss group following an hour or so behind. Two weeks later we heard that seventeen rounds had been fired into the back of their bus while departing the checkpoint. No one was hurt.*

At nightfall we were descending into the Amazon Basin. At one point the road became a vague path, requiring a guide with a flashlight to lead the way on foot. Later the vehicle came to an abrupt halt. To Chando's shout the driver answered that a lone gunman had appeared in the headlights. Chando opened the front door and after a few words threw out a handful of coins as we started on. He confided that the driver would be fired for stopping; that with all the luggage and equipment packed inside the back of the bus, gunshots would have done no harm. The rogue rebel was an isolated remnant of the insurrection brought down, for the most part, by the unyielding efforts of one man:

On the eve of the last Presidential election in Peru I listened to the persuasive rhetoric of the urbane novelist, Mario Vargas Llosa, as he spoke from a podium high above the plaza of his hometown, Arequipa. He was rumored to have the backing of the U.S. and I would have bet on his victory. Afterwards, I watched other candidates rant on my hotel room television. And then there appeared a mild-mannered Japanese man, Alberto Fujimori, a schoolteacher and engineer. On the adobe walls of small towns the slogan "Vota por El Chinito" had been repeatedly hand painted. Rural Peruvians knew of the Chinese, but had never seen anyone from Japan. Disgusted with violence and weary of economic chaos, the people of Peru elected the "Little Chinaman," rejecting the wealthy oligarchy of Lima that came to relentlessly oppose his every move. Fujimori crushed the Shining Path and brought financial

*stability. He was eventually corrupted by one of his military staff.
His second-term re-election was met with doubt and contempt.
At the Lima airport I watched split live images on a coffee shop
television screen. On one side was the decorous slow gavotte of
the inauguration. On the other were scenes of the streets filled
with rioters, and then pictures of protesters throwing lit Molotov
cocktails through windows in the Palace of Justice.*

We watched for hours from the riverbank of the Tambopata
as the rubber rafts were first inflated and then carefully loaded.
Three would take participants, with the fourth bearing our cargo.
Pepe passed among the group selecting those to man a specific
raft. Always the egalitarian, I objected, but was overruled by the
crew. Later I would learn the reason.

On the second day on the river soldiers on the Bolivian
shore hailed us and waved us over. We moved on by as the guides
explained that their motive was to extort a "government tax."

We anticipated easy Class III and Class IV rapids. Unknown
to us, the rains were coming early to the Tambopata.

By the third day we were hurtling through almost continuous Class V and VI rapids. At one point all four rafts were
moving swiftly along upside down and surrounded by a scat-
tering of helmets bobbing like red M&Ms.

Our yellow, Italian-made raft was longer than the others.
Lucho had gone forward to give commands as we sped through
some of the fastest water thus far, leaving me in the stern. As
we dropped into a steep whirlpool, the raft buckled, catapulting
me over the others and into the river. I am not a strong swim-
mer, and like a fool I had vainly left the life vest straps loose
over my belly. Moving fast, I could not see anything above the
waves except large rocks rushing by. I imagined I would be
smashed or drowned.

Soon I could hear shouts. Pepe was in the bow paddling
like a madman, leading the strong crew he had selected for the
rescue raft. The current had stripped me naked except for the

life vest by which they hauled me aboard. Liza, an emergency room nurse, said I was blue, and that her hospital had "coded" patients who looked better than I.

Liza was the guides' favorite. They called her *Picaflor* (hummingbird). A large tarp was set up as shelter from the continuous rain. Each morning we would stand under it and eat bowls of oatmeal that we flavored individually by adding instant coffee, powdered cocoa, powdered creamer, and/or sugar. One night the captains presented Liza with a birthday cake, baked under the most adverse conditions imaginable. There was a surgeon along who incessantly chattered in her ear at every stop, to her seeming indifference. We felt sorry for both of them.

Within a week of our return home they were married. Within a year they were divorced.

That night, as the river rose, Chando unzipped each tent and reached inside to check the floor for wetness. One high-strung codger, who should not have been along, awoke and screamed, "Get out! I don't know what you're called here, but in America you're a queer. Get out!" In the dark the guides cleared higher ground with machetes. Mendel severed one of his fingertips and cut another to the bone in the process. Under the tarp by the rays of an intense light, the surgeon, the nurse, and a cardiologist sewed the wounds without benefit of anesthesia. The next morning the bandages were reapplied so that Mendel could paddle. In Cuzco he expressed relief that the medics were along, "Otherwise Chando would have done it, and I would look like Frankenstein!"

The next day Chando decided that we must stop while he and Mendel scouted the rapids ahead. As soon as they were out of sight the remaining guides approached me asking that I intercede and ask Chando to go no farther. Their request was unusual to say the least. As the client, such decisions were not mine to make. A skeptic would say the protest was fear driven. I knew better. I told them I could not intervene. The guides began to unload the rafts to make manifest their objections. I told Lucho to leave ours alone. He came later to say that his peers declared that if he did not unload he would be called a "cocksucker" and would have to eat under the table. I gave in. Chando returned to say we would not leave. All were relieved. The mutiny was never mentioned.

Some were clad in wet, dirty long underwear as we sat all afternoon staring at the river. Now and then the current would undermine a tree on the banks. For the first time since we put in, the insects were ferocious. We could not stay indefinitely as we had a specific rendezvous with motorized dugouts to take us on the last days of calm water. Fortunately the rain stopped and the sun came out; it was glorious. The dugouts were long and narrow with canopies of fronds. One had a small propane stove mounted in the bow, on which pancakes were being prepared. A retired doctor told us to "get those *niños* to hurry up breakfast." Jon commented that such undeserved assumptions of entitlement were the cause of many world problems, and suggested we throw the doctor overboard. At dusk we saw a jaguar drinking on the riverbank. Later a capybara also came down to drink.

Awaiting us were open stilted platforms with rows of mattresses, clean sheets, and mosquito netting. A couple of brilliant birds hung from the thatch. We were overcome with joy. A British Broadcasting Company crew was camped nearby and had erected towers for filming a unique phenomenon. Each morning thousands of macaws flocked to a bank of cliffs to eat the clay that counteracts the acid of their fruit diet. The filming disruption caused the birds to move just far enough downstream to be out of camera range.

The next day we put ashore at Puerto Maldonado, a rough gold mining town inaccessible by road and the setting of Peter Matthiessen's *At Play in the Fields of the Lord.* The "tourist hotel" was the best in town. Its screens were rusted and ripped, and cold water belched from a headless shower pipe. To us it was palatial.

At dinner time a line of young women stood under a banner in the lobby that read "Miss Amazonia Contest." They all had large brown eyes and an abundance of long black hair. They were unsteady in high heels, and their sexuality was as inherent as their breathing.

The next morning pedicabs took us to the airport for what was to have been a charter flight, but became the first scheduled flight on that route by a fledgling airline. Its name was being painted behind a small counter, which we crowded around while locals were handed packets for delivery in Cuzco.

The airplane's interior was bare metal, with continuous canvas benches facing each other across piles of cargo secured by nets, on which squatted extra passengers. On one wall, a large rectangle was defined by rough painted dashes. The same hand had painted EMERGENCY—CUT WITH AXE. The overburdened plane lifted laboriously into the air and flew low over a rough jungle canopy from which a thin fog was rising.

∿∿∿

Of the twenty on the trip, all but four came to travel with us again and again.

∿∿∿

Spread on a chair across the room is a faded purple T-shirt. Over the heart are two small crossed paddles and the words "HIGHSIDE CLUB, CUZCO, PERU." On the back, cracked yellow paint depicts a rising sun eclipsed by the spread wings of a giant condor. And below is inscribed, "RAFTING IN THE TIME OF CHOLERA, TAMBOPATA RIVER EXPEDITION, 1992."

∿∿∿

The risks, the friends, the memories of Peru are endless: They all exist because one Sunday afternoon, thirty-seven years ago, I stopped by a friend's house.

Avalanche

There are some things one would rather have done than do.

Edward Abbey

O UR HEROES FALL as the years go by. Most do not topple over clay feet, but sink under the burden of imagined virtues we have ascribed.

Marco Cruz is still standing.

I had read that he was "the best and most expensive climbing guide in South America." He cut his crampons on glaciers that line *The Avenue of the Volcanoes* in his native Ecuador. At twelve years of age he climbed Chimborazo, the highest peak in Ecuador. He was also hired as help for an Italian team's attempt to scale challenging El Altar, a wedge of ice pointing up from rolling forests. When the team leader became seriously ill, Marco took charge and is credited with being the first Ecuadorian to ascend to the summit of El Altar.

He went on to successes in every major range in the world, and became admired also for his quiet confidence and modesty. Men invariably envy him for his intelligent, beautiful wife, his partner in every way.

I have a picture of him taken in his home/office, standing before a stuffed condor with a wingspan that fills the room. On the wall is one of his mountain photos, many of which have been published. They silently chronicle the rapid melting of the world's mammoth ice masses. On a table lies a large volume about *ayahuasca* that includes an image of Marco, eyes rolled back, under the influence of the powerful hallucinogen from the Upper Amazon. *That the complex formula for its preparation evolved among obscure ethnic groups that lead simple lives has puzzled anthropologists and biochemists, and is a compelling argument that escaping reality is a universal need.*

Condor Adventures engaged Marco, assisted by the head of the German national mountain climbing club, to guide us up Illiniza North (16,785 feet), Cotopaxi (19,348 feet), and Chimborazo (20,703 feet), which rises behind his home. We were eight proud beginners in new, hard-shell, "extreme" boots designed to accommodate clamp-on crampons.

Camping under Illiniza, we countered insomnia resulting from anxiety and altitude with Dalmane, a tranquilizer/sedative. After dark the red neon lava flow on Mount Sangay could be seen in the distance. According to Marco, after a long approach through dense jungle, Sangay was "an easy climb after you passed the 'bums,'" meaning "bombs"—molten globs that rained down at a certain level.

Early morning brought a Quechua woman leading a cow and offering raw milk from a large bucket. I was able to stop the first customer from raising the dipper to her lips. Anything *crudo* ("fresh, uncooked") might be desirable at the health food store, but is dangerous in the wild.

The climb of Illiniza North was just a rigorous hike with, as always, a weary descent on fatigued legs.

Cotopaxi is a perfect cone of black scree topped by a deep snowcap, similar to Mount Fuji. At the refuge just below the ice, the women's faces were puffed with oxygen deprivation, and they decided to go no farther. The battered building was cavernous, but that night it sheltered only our group and two Scots, who traded their Spartan porridge for some of our freeze-dried meals, which they proclaimed delicious.

At 1:00 AM we started up. Before mounting the glacier lip I broke through a small snow bridge, sinking thigh deep in ice water. Soon a sound like a muffled shotgun blast caused the surface to shrug. Later, I realized that it was a large mass breaking free. At first light our spiral route changed to ascend directly up the slope. One of our team started down. Of two groups, ours was the slower. When the others, led by the German, passed us on their way down, Marco advised that we would turn around if we did not attain the crater soon. We made it to the rim of the white biomorphic orifice, then reversed our path.

Halfway down, everything under us gave way with a roar. In a second, images of avalanche cords, avalanche wands, broken necks, lungs vacuumed of air, all flashed before my mind's eye. I was a baby tumbling in battering surf, instinctively swimming upward as the ropes pulled my torso in a tug-of-war.

Then, it stopped.

First came the awareness of still being alive, followed by the conviction that all my bones were broken. Finding that to be false, I struggled toward the dim, diffused light from above. The others were digging out nearby. The 11 millimeter umbilicals were intact. The lower group was in disarray. They had watched in horror as the dislodged snow mass swept down upon them. The German miscounted his charges and panicked, thinking one of them was buried. Marco, ever calm, led us from the downside of one boulder after another, concerned about aftershocks. I noticed wet eyes as he spoke to his brother, at the refuge, by walkie-talkie. Later I heard about his losing a boyhood friend to a similar disaster when they were climbing together. A rather abrasive young attorney speculated that our leader was calling for rescue helicopters. *If* the Ecuadorian military had such equipment, they certainly would not deploy it to pluck novice climbers from comparatively easy slopes.

We later learned that our route had been obliterated and was no longer used, and that a couple of our ice axes and a camera had been found at the base.

Steve had several broken ribs and some of Blake's skin had been flayed from his upper body. I accompanied them on the long night's ride to Quito's main hospital. The others stayed back to hike around the base of Chimborazo, rather than attempt the ascent.

Our reunion with others for whom Condor Adventures had provided a cruise of the Galapagos Islands during our climbs was exuberant with the elation that comes from having triumphed. (Did not William Faulkner write that to survive *is* to triumph?) We feasted on shellfish bubbling in butter and spices that spilled over the rim of deep platters at *Las Redes* restaurant in Quito.

The next day was cloudy and rather depressing as we met in a hotel room where "Lizard," a bodybuilder, schemed to bring back anabolic steroids to his acquaintances at the gym. U.S. pharmaceutical corporations manufacture drugs in Latin America and sell them there, often without requiring prescriptions, for a small percentage of their cost in the United States. Dean, a wealthy businessman, wanted no part of the venture, but could not help giving marketing advice and profit projections.

Lizard went down later and mailed some of the product home, concealed in toy police cars.

Across the street an overhead door slammed down with a crash. We were jolted enough to spill drinks.

Such hypersensitivity to cataclysmic noises soon passed.

The humility is still with us.

Recently Paula Dorney, climbing alone except for one of Marco's guides, went to the top of Cotopaxi and back in six hours, three less than it took us with the unexpected ride down.

She is a heroine who is still standing.

THE AUSTRALIAN

O Western Wind, when wilt thou blow,
That the little rains down may rain?
Christ! That I were in my bed
And my love were in my arms again.

Anonymous

T 22,841 FEET, *Aconcagua, on the Chilean/Argentine border, is the highest peak in the Western Hemisphere. More climbers have died on its slopes than on Everest and* K-2 *combined. Experienced mountaineers do not consider the* Ruta Normal *difficult.*

It was silent. Few climbers were outside their tents in the cold clear night. The mules (after which this desolate base camp, *Plaza de Mulas,* was named) had gone back down earlier in the day, driven fast and hard by the loud *arrieros,* men with smooth, tanned skin stretched tight across large hands and broad faces, the Argentine descendents of the raucous Iberians who raped Quixote's Dulcinea. There is a kinship of work that transcends nationality: Except for hats with upturned brims, the *bombacho* pants, and the wide sashes, these were the donkey drovers of Santorini.

The weather was better than the year we had spent fifteen days on the mountain and failed; but everyone in that carnival of nylon that would never stop popping in the wind was sick.

Those coming down were sick with exhaustion. Those going up were sick from the altitude. And there were a few, who had not known the enormity of what now confronted them, who were sick with fear.

David, a medical school student and our reserve guide, was in demand for consultation. Before we reached base camp a climber had shown him what was left of his toes. (We were assured that only a couple would have to be removed.) As the climber tried to put his sock back on I asked, *"¿Cumbre?"* without arrogance. He answered, *"No,"* without shame. Those descending *had* to be asked if they had summited. It was expected. What was never asked was *why* they had not. The reasons were too complex, and no one really knew. Those who tried to explain were of the excuse breed, a rare species at that elevation.

There are common characteristics in the faces of those who have spent a long time striving for a peak. They identify them and set them apart. The prolonged focusing of will gives a fixed stricture to the muscles of the cheeks and jaw. The eyes go deep and hollow and stare at a place no one else can see.

There was some levity among those camped on that gritty lunar landscape, but it was soldier's humor: bizarre, macabre.

On the second dull afternoon, sounds of astonishment moved across the village of wind-whipped, gumball-colored tents. With effort, I rolled over and unzipped the flap. Striding through were two figures that must have been carried up by mules. One was globular in a puffy green parka with the 7-UP logo, another a cameraman filming us wretches as we reached for the emerald two-liter bottles handed out by the soda pop Santa Claus. *Six months later in a starkly modern Madrid apartment, a glossy woman in a black chiffon Dolce and Gabbana dress and stilettos would call out, "¡Mi Amor! Mira, mira; what a commercial. It is so realistic."*

Among the hundred or so of us camped at *Plaza de Mulas* there were two large teams. All we saw of one was their crates with CANADA stenciled on the canvas covers and the maple-leaf flag. Their higher camp was barely discernable through binoculars.

We had heard about the other team, the Australians. That the famous John Muir was with them, and had returned from the top three times as the rest slowly made their way up. How they had compromised their schedule to rescue a German climber from a crevasse; he had been assumed dead and abandoned by his countrymen. It could have been a rumor. But a rumor is a lie, and lying, like bathing, was an indulgence left below.

We moved up. The weather let it be easier this time.

As we slogged ahead I multiplied the height of various peaks by 3.281, converting meters to feet to take my mind away from my body. I thought of the previous attempt:

The hope of getting to the top on my fiftieth birthday: For lack of a piss bottle, having to go outside at 3:00 AM. For lack of an insulated canteen cover, the startle of little ice flakes crisp against my teeth after I had already swallowed, my core resisting the ingested cold until Nido de Condores, *where I entered the womb of the forgiving Marmot bag, shaking violently until it held enough heat to take me to the tropics.* Man has not been able to produce a substance that provides as much insulation per weight as down from the neck of the Gray Goose. I had paid an additional fifty dollars for an extra three ounces to be added to the model originally rated to -30 degrees Fahrenheit, thus bringing it down to -50 degrees. We joked about a billboard with us nude on a peak, holding our bags and crying, "I want my Marmie!" *Descending from our failure I became exasperated each time Ben blamed the guides, the weather, the pace, anything but our lack of strength and will. When he remarked within earshot of our English-speaking guides—they who had treated us with such patience and concern—that they were hurrying us in order to come back with their next clients, I threatened to put my ice-axe through his chest. Pounding the final twenty-seven miles the last day, I tried to keep up with Blake's long-strided pace as best I could while supporting David, whose legs were shot. The last stretch: highway pavement then right through the big double doors of the lodge, contemptuous of the tourists in the dining room, and on into the warm, secure wood-paneled bar, drinking what we agreed was the best beer of our lives and laughing at the two framed photographs. One was of Reinhold Messner, arguably the best climber in the world, grinning through an icy beard, one hand gloveless from having pressed the delayed shutter button, as he stood on one of the fourteen highest peaks in the world (those over 8,000 meters, 26,240 feet). He soon became the first to solo them all.*

The other photograph was of Marilyn Monroe. She seemed pleased to see us.

Berlin Camp has the "highest permanent dwellings in the world": two miserable wooden lean-tos at an elevation that cannot support plant or human life. From there we began our summit assault in the middle of the night. The black and white moonscape had an abstract eeriness in the light of the full moon, around which we had planned our ascent. The scythes of snow were brilliant against dark scree.

Eventually we reached the *Canaleta,* a steep concave boulder field some 300 feet wide and 1,500 feet long. Its surface was thousands of smooth, round boulders from the size of basketballs to that of small cars. Most were unstable and tended to roll or slip as you placed your weight upon them. Much of the field had to be navigated on hands and knees. At 21,000 feet the lack of oxygen made this a slow, difficult job.

Blake was far ahead. Mark and I were side-by-side. At that point in our lives I had more high-altitude experience, although he was a natural athlete in excellent condition. Health and fitness were his hobbies, and sports were his pleasures. I constantly cautioned him against going too fast. This was out of selfishness, knowing that I would be more determined if not left behind. I could not believe it when he suddenly declared he was going down. It occurred to me he might be joking. He said he was extremely disoriented and in a moment he was gone. (After two nights at base camp he summited rapidly. At thirty-five he retired from brokering bonds and went on to become a mountaineering instructor and the best climber any of us have known.)

The gains in the *Canaleta* came so slowly I was not aware of making any progress at all. I had noticed someone at about my level an hour before. He did not seem to have moved. It took most of the day to get above this obstacle course. Two men and a woman traversed the summit ridge just in front of me. Dropping to our right was a sheer steep snow face, the South Wall, known locally as *"Pala Messner,"* Messner's Shovel. Two years before he had forced a new route up its concave surface.

At the summit there was a feeling of exhilaration and relief. But it is not there that the surge of triumph comes to you. There is only nausea, fatigue, and the sense of expenditure of something vague and indefinable, of which there is a limited supply: Something not to be regained. Nor does the elation come as you leave the mountain but later, when, after a warm shower and clean sheets, you go out to meet the day and breakfast and there is a feeling of wellbeing so intense that it seems to amplify every sense.

As I started down over the boulders, my weakness became the only reality. The larger stones would shift and the smaller ones would roll and there was not enough strength left in my legs to compensate. It was increasingly more difficult to recover from each slip or fall. A dry cough had become more frequent and severe.

I became aware of dusk about the same time I realized that I was alone in the *Canaleta*. I could no longer afford time to rest, nor was I able to move any faster.

Just before total darkness, I noticed the silhouette of what could have been an oddly configured stack of stones, far below at the end of the rock fall. When I finally reached that point it had been ten hours since I entered the garden of stones. The shape rose, turned to me, and said, "I could see that someone was still up there. I thought I would see you down." It was one of the Australians.

This person that I had not met before walked alongside as I stumbled through endless patterns of light and dark, forms and planes, flashes and voids. At one point he said, "That cough is rough, we have a doctor at Berlin." The night lasted for days and days as I performed a slow mad dance among the streaks of white. Years later we came to the tents. The Australian stopped at one and mentioned my condition. A muffled reply advised that I come by tomorrow. Tomorrow, I hoped, I would be below and warm.

As he fell into his tent I stood there, lacking thanks. I took off my big down parka and threw it through the flap behind him, saying that I wanted him to have it, then staggered away.

The morning was dazzlingly bright. Long lanes of ice and snow ran ahead of us. I fell behind and lost the trail, dehydrated, with the thin thread of victory held taut inside. I approached a group and asked for some water, and for help in finding my way down. One motioned to another saying, "He is starting now. You can go with him." I knew I could not keep up, so after locating the trail I went over the side and down, down, down, the ice and snow turning to dirt, the dirt turning to dust. And then I could see the tiny beads of color below: the tents of *Plaza de Mulas*.

∽∽∽

It was silent. In the darkness a new year was quietly born. There were a few shouts of *¡Felíz!* and *¡Salud!* from the Spanish team. Then silence again. And then a song swelled slowly on the still night air: "*Waltzing Matilda, Waltzing Matilda, You'll come a-waltzing Matilda with me…*" And one of those voices belonged to a man I had never seen in the light, and without whom I would not have been there to listen.

An Appreciation:
"You're Not the Boss of Me!"

I've decided [she] is bionic and teflonic.
Being banged around and scraped over multiple surfaces
does not seem to impact her unduly.

Muriel Lindsay

A S SHE STEPPED across the avenue, spirited and long-legged as a young colt, her glance was so brief and indifferent that my friend consoled, "She is way past twenty-one, and she is not saving it for anybody." He was wrong. Her reverence for passion is so extreme that she never speaks of it, or uses it as the currency of social commerce as do so many.

She had managed sales for a small boutique since its inception: Well-chosen *avant-garde* fashions, purchased with the credit cards of greed-bleakened fathers and husbands as a way to control their dependents. Through curiosity and a genuine interest in people, she developed an uncanny ability to sell. When employed by a large department store, she would pre-select garments for appointments with local celebrities and businesswomen, and sometimes registered sales of $3,000 within an hour!

The little shop thrived under her firm, even hand. Attractive customers and free champagne drew men to the Saturday morning festivities on the premises. After they bumped the "wiggle shelves" or distracted the "living mannequins" or spilled Chandon on the merchandise, they were asked to leave. She held them in high regard, so there was no animosity. Her scale of merit for such allegiances is based solely upon the recipient's lack of guile and pretense. Those who measure up, she always defends. On the contrary, her threshold of tolerance for sham, hypocrisy, or elitism is so low that those who cross it are met with a contempt that is severe, relentless, and unyielding.

Her clumsiness (and total disregard for its consequences) is legend. At the store's opening she asked, "What's this?" and pushed a button. Within minutes the municipal S.W.A.T. team had leveled shotguns at the plate glass. Over an employee's background music tape she accidentally recorded herself making fun of the owner, and ran to the player as it came over the speakers. Days later she, incredibly, did it again, with her telling about the previous incident. Helen Gurley Brown once warned her readers ("Camaro chicks" hoping to buy sophistication for the price of a *Cosmopolitan)* that a man who has block and plank bookshelves or a mattress on the floor was not a good marriage prospect. The first night she came over, the foot of the bed was so near the stereo that she kicked enough buttons to render it forever useless. Physical damage comes to her with a frequency that is serial. Thanks to whatever gods there are, she is indestructible. Recently she fell from a runaway horse in the Andes and broke her arm. In an upper body cast she returned to her responsibilities as group leader. Even had we been able to afford it, she would have refused the pin-setting surgery the orthopedist insisted upon. When a friend who was there heard this, he was incredulous, "Didn't you see the x-rays?! Didn't you see the *X*-rays?!" The bones have knit, but she says she could not bowl, even if she wanted to.

As a business partner she is often disconcerting. Her stubborn, silent mantra is, "You're not the boss of me!" She reminds me of someone's comment about his girlfriend, "She would live with me on a small sailboat, or hike through the jungle at a moment's notice, but she can't balance a checkbook," to which a woman friend commented, "Well… those kinds of apples taste that way." Often, she bears the brunt of blame that should be mine, playing "bad cop" to my "good cop." Invariably, when I remove someone from our mailing list (about the same as being asked to leave Krystal, or being dropped from the Book-of-the-Month Club) within weeks there comes a call: "I didn't receive information about your next adventure. I know *she* took me off the list! Please put me back on." The irony and the frequency with which it happens are absurd.

I have never known her to betray any principle of behavior to which she subscribes. She has, unconsciously, cultivated a durable shield to mask a care and concern for the well-being of every living thing, whether animal, child, or adult, especially the most weak and vulnerable.

Her first name is biblical and her last name Irish, but her middle name is spelled: L-O-Y-A-L-T-Y.

She is the sister I never had, and the friend who has provoked strength from where I thought I had none.

In Praise of the Landlady

She's got diamonds on the soles of her shoes.

Paul Simon

A S SHE MOVED the lock of hair away from her forehead, I noticed that her eyes were exactly the color of the emerald baguette on her right hand. When she asked if I would like to see the place, I said I had been the architect.

Thirty-eight years before, by utilizing innovative methods to simplify construction and reduce labor costs, the two book-matched, detached dwellings had been built for less than fifteen dollars per square foot and were nominated for a national design award. I had been the first tenant, with our studio downstairs and my living quarters above, and I had just decided to live there again.

When I mentioned the landlady's eyes and only her first name, Debbie, my business partner, recognized her at once. She is well known and admired in our small town.

Site planning was difficult for the place, as we were determined to preserve the many ancient oaks that studded the long, narrow parcel. She has filled the remaining surfaces with sub-tropical plants that seem to grow wild, but are nurtured with constant care. Occasionally, in high heels, she will rip down a wayward vine or dead limb.

One Saturday morning, forgetting the grounds had been selected for the "Parade of Gardens," I stumbled downstairs in undershorts to find the house surrounded. Some visitors were peering through the plate glass windows.

Each noon the landlady drives her white Mercedes Benz with the day's trash (often empty shoeboxes) on the trunk, eighty feet to the street, turns around, and drives back home. Her home includes a private garden and a series of decks that step down to the small stream beyond.

Like the Batmobile, at dusk the sleek vehicle slowly prowls out, bound for Park Plaza Gardens, Luma, or the Wine Room.

She is glamorous, with a touch of Partonesque earthiness as a counterpoint that makes the polish glow even more. She is charming, friendly and cheerful. Women often ask me her age. Who knows? Who cares?!

Upon seeing the landlady, Debbie quoted the Panamanian woman who comes to clean, as exclaiming, "Whooo-eee! She sexy. I bet Uncle would like to boom-boom that." I asked who "Uncle" was. Debbie said, "Who do you think?"

My bedroom balcony, shaded from the weather, thrusts into the treetops. The network of limbs houses a world of creatures: Sometimes large birds of prey, often tiny sparrows, and always lizards of every subspecies. There is a plethora of squirrels that snack on bromeliad blossoms and seem embarrassed when they miss a long jump. A five-foot black snake lives in the pavers by the front door.

I start each morning with a mug of Café Bustelo on the balcony, reading from "Leaves of Grass" or "The Dhammapada" with, perhaps, Beethoven's Fifth Piano Concerto in the background. The workday closes with a large goblet of Chilean merlot, sipped in silence.

~~~

I am fortunate for the place where I live, and for she who holds it in her hands.

La Habana, La Enigma

I've been lied to for forty years.

Dr. James Easterling

THE MIAMI HERALD: *"...on returning from his fraterni-ty's Leadership School at Northwestern University, Buz was met by Tom and Ted. The three friends then flew to Havana for a holiday in the tropics. ..."* The text on the society page was accompanied by a headshot of a crew-cutted youth with a hint of smugness in his eye, so common in men of his age. He thought then that he knew everything about women; he found instead that each day he knew less, and eventually realized that he knew nothing—that each woman is a unique and insoluble mystery; that all he can do is present himself unembellished. And hope.

A fat Cadillac taxi with driver to match rolls through red clay fields that remind him of his family's place in the Blue Ridge foothills. Entering the city an olfactory signature is imprinted: a fusion of tobacco, perfume, and rotting fruit that would always say, "Havana," just as surely as the smell of wet wool and urine would say, "Cuzco." Directly from the airport, driving past one mansion after another after another, each patio with exotic plants and women in lingerie and high heels, with hair like night flowing over bare shoulders. Places to chat and to choose. Down the broad Malecon, the constant breeze blowing spray over the seawall, maintaining the algal slickness of the promenade. Two blocks inland from the magnificent equestrian statue of Antonio Maceo is the Hotel Diana. Tres matrimoniales. The bumpkins, all architects-to-be, remark on the four-fixture baths. Roaring laughter, a shriek and a giggle, a redheaded giant in only a Florida Gators T-shirt is seen running down the hall with a naked woman on his shoulders.

Breakfast at Café Daytona. The Man of the World orders in halting Spanish. The waiter shouts in perfect English, "Three coffees! They want milk in them." Late morning at the art deco Bacardi Building, bat logos on the façade, businessmen and cops shoulder-to-shoulder at the mezzanine bar; endless free daiquiris in slotted paper coasters. In traffic, the cabbie hails a tall shirtless mulatto who waves back: "Superman," a celebrity known even to blushing Coral Gables High grads.

In the early morning dark, distant explosions are heard. She whispers in his ear, *"Revolución."*

≈≈≈

And they cross the Gulfstream: Talented young Cuban architects working for junior draftsmen's wages, their employers gloating that they can hire two for the price of one. Worldly gentlemen, chiding their Argentine colleague about ordering a "Whooper" for lunch. Walk-up coffee windows open onto S.W. Eighth Street (eventually "Calle Ocho"). In 1924, his grandfather had purchased twenty-two acres on the corner of the street and Le Jeune Road: Sullivan's Riding Academy.

He comes to know a woman with an apartment near the Orange Bowl, who, with her jai-alai player boyfriend, had been guests of the Hemingways. Another in the backseat at Crandon Park, "How you like my mouse?" "Your what?!" "My mouse."

~~~

When I return with two others, they ask the Cuban Consul in Merida if there might be problems, she replies, "There will not be with my country; there might be with yours."

The whores: gone. The casinos: gone. The aristocrats: gone. The Tropicana: flourishing, still with its entrance fountain of eight white marble nudes cavorting around the rim. A handshake and a cigar for the men, a kiss on the cheek and a rose for the women; a hundred tables under the stars on which white-gloved waiters place bottles of fine rum and fill champagne flutes. The most beautiful dancers imaginable perform to a sixty-four-piece orchestra, with a show every night since 1939 (except for two nights during World War II). Fantasy costumes, impeccable, not a run or a loose thread; plumes, bustiers, waist-high yellow leggings with the entire bottoms deleted. This was the show that every bloated Las Vegas revue would attempt to imitate. At La Bodeguita del Medio, under Hemingway's quote, dignified waiters in guayaberas serve mojitos to somber Russian soldiers with mulatas on their arms. Decades later, his guide would be Olga, an airport official: Yuri. There are no two Western cultures more opposite in every aspect—a political marriage made in hell. The few Cuban soldiers on the streets wear the epaulets of the special force to repel an invasion from the North.

The buildings of Habana Vieja have begun to decay. Only a few colonial structures have been renovated, but the attention to detail has been meticulous down to every tiny mosaic tile and each slender wrought iron tendril. A children's dance class giggles and poses before boarding a decrepit bus. That afternoon their adult counterparts are observed rehearsing outdoors at Marina Hemingway; their skin tones are an even gradation from flan to espresso. On the Prado, I offer a U.S. dollar to pay for coffee. The vendor places his hands on the counter, closes his eyes, and bows his head. Those in line fall silent. One nods, then leads me down the street and around the corner to a doorway, counts out pesos, puts the bill in his mouth, and runs. The baroque former Presidential Palace, where the dictator thwarted a coup by hiding in the dumbwaiter, is now the Museum of the Revolution. On each corner of the grand staircase are marble busts: Simon Bolivar, Benito Juarez, Jose Marti, and Abraham Lincoln. From the vaulted ceiling of the great hall hangs a mammoth crystal chandelier. The walls are mirrored except for the one with high arched windows that look out upon the harbor. Seen from the mezzanine above, naval cadets in dress whites form a slow whirlpool, the vortex being a lone midshipwoman. Showcases on the upper floor display implements of torture from the Batista regime; the famous New York Times news photo of Fidel with troops in the Sierra Maestra, which stifled rumors of his death; a captured strategic map of the failed Bay of Pigs invasion; a photograph of the bodies of two women strafed by the attack while on the way to work in the fields.

We ride old wooden coaches on the canecutter's train to Veradero, to dine on lobster at a bland beachfront hotel that could have been in any fading town on Florida's Coast. Outside the bus station I approach a man with a family about buying pesos. In reply, he turns to the ocean, shakes his fist and yells a political slogan in the direction of Key West. The ticket taker stops me from boarding the bus because I am wearing shorts. The waiting room crowd protests. One man jabs his finger and shouts that there is no such rule; that I am being discriminated against because I am from the United States. The official says it is a new rule, but he appears intimidated. As a guard approaches, a young man offers sweatpants from a gym bag. As I struggle into the small garment, everyone laughs and applauds. Aboard, an elderly lady indicates that the driver is watching and that I should not shed the pants until the interior lights are off.

The night is so dark that only thought has form and substance, except in the far distance, a small elusive glow teases the void: La Habana.

∾∾∾

Returning again, the Russians: gone (a bandleader jokes, "Bye, bye, polka!"). Consumer goods: gone. The economy: shot to hell. Pretty young women trade their *culitos* for hotel room toiletries and U.S. dollars.

With the collusion of the dictator Fulgencio Batista, U.S. criminals had controlled a vast network of whorehouses in Havana, supported by North American tourists, many of them politicians, writers, and entertainment celebrities. Fidel Castro's government abolished them all, along with gambling and drug trafficking. The casinos and narcotics have not been allowed to return, but the economic hardship resulting from the collapse of the Soviet Union caused many women to freelance the streets to pay for scarce consumer goods. The Party philosophy is that it is a woman's right to do with her body as she chooses, but exploiters such as pimps and madams are severely punished. With the recent rapid increase in international tourism bolstering the economy, such commerce is becoming less compelling.

Young men sell pilfered Cohibas and Montecristos, US$50 a box, and offer illicit transport in dilapidated '57 Chevrolets. At the Hotel Nacional, photos of guests: Frank Sinatra, Sir Winston Churchill, Meyer Lansky with bodyguard, and Naomi Campbell adorn the walls. (Recently Pope John Paul II and the Baltimore Orioles were added.) Music is everywhere. Jon bares his shoulder to the band, revealing the image by Korda that has been stenciled on walls the world over. They break into song, the lyrics, the closing of their martyr's final letter: "*...Hasta Siempre, Comandante Che Guevara.*"

The roof garden of the Hotel Ambos Mundos (Hemingway's trysting place) offers sunset cocktails and a panorama of the city. The façade of the old cathedral glows with tiny lights (the churches have never closed). At Café Paris, heels hit a tabletop like a pistol shot. The dancer, in a fringed *microminifalda*, hands down a note on a paper scrap. A few blocks away, a doctor's

family sits together in their living room; their bedroom, furnished with Valentine pillows, is rented by the hour.

∾∾∾

And again: Income from tourism has eclipsed that of
tobacco and sugar, causing concern that its promotion will
take priority over education and health care. Calle Obispo
is crowded with Europeans. Art galleries, a pet beauty salon,
and a lavishly appointed optician's line the street, between
apartments with no water or electricity. A grand old coquina
structure has become the elegant Hotel Florida. CNN, BBC,
and *The Sopranos* can be seen on television screens in lobbies
and bars. The convertible peso has been pegged to the U.S.
dollar. Cubans, now allowed to hold all currencies, mix with
visitors everywhere. La Lluvia de Oro could be Key West's
Sloppy Joe's in the 1940s. Our guide has been required to take
postgraduate courses in history, architecture, and languages.
A heroic statue sits on the steps of a university building, the
artist's conception of the perfect woman: the face of an adolescent, the body of a mature *mulata*… with a mother's hands.
Bright yellow fiberglass "coconuts" with scooter mechanisms
provide short rides. Student drivers always ask about our country, and always say that to go there is their *sueño*, their dream.

∾∾∾

Many visits later, we fly in: Fidel Castro has just been hospi-
talized and a hurricane has brushed the island. *The Miami Herald*
quotes Condoleezza Rice as saying that tension is running high on
the streets of Havana; that the military is everywhere. Condoleezza
lies. The only soldiers seen are the honor guard at the American
Interests Section. Government secretaries having lunch or pick-
ing out lipsticks wear the only other uniforms; the exception is
the Tourist Police, who seem to be on every corner in the Old
City. They wear gray berets, carry nightsticks and walkie-talkies,

and are resented by all concerned. One of our senators (who co-sponsored the legislation creating the embargo) complained that his visit was marred by the solicitations of young women offering favors and men offering illicit transport and cigars. The Party responded by creating this force, whose only duty is to insulate the tourists from those hoping to earn additional currency.

The euro is now preferred. The dollar can only be exchanged at a 20% penalty. *El Centro* has become a slum—broken pavement and broken dreams; everything is broken. A new life-size bronze of *"Ernesto"* leans forward from his favorite stool at La Floridita, "The Cradle of the Daiquiri." A "Papa" (half the sugar, twice the rum) has gone up to US$9. The transport of choice is a faux-antique open touring car, painted as a Checker cab. The driver may keep all her fares over US$150 per day. On New Year's Eve Day there are lines at dress shops and beauty salons.

Along the airport road: apartments for the impoverished of three Andean nations as they await the *milagro* of eye surgery.

∾∾∾

Two years ago: the lobster Obispo, splayed and swollen, crowded the garlic shrimp, rice, and black beans on the large platter (costing little more than a bucket of KFC). Our patio table was close to the musicians and the grand piano. The singer looked fragile, but her voice was clear and strong. The linguist among us overheard that the Buena Vista Social Club was to perform in two hours at the National Theater. We rushed there to find it closed. On to the *other* National Theater by the Plaza of the Revolution, only to find it dark, too. On to the Hotel Nacional, hoping for information. *Eureka!* (I found it!) We hurried through the lobby that could have been designed by Addison Mizner, architect of The Breakers, the Kennedy home, and the Dodge family mansion, who came to Palm Beach in a Rolls Royce Silver Cloud with hardly a cent in his pocket and shed some grace on what would have otherwise become another tasteless enclave of the wealthy. Passing the white marble nude under the lone-star flag that never flew over Texas, we entered a cavernous space aglow with white linen, crystal, and silver. The Buena Vista Social Club was just beginning. The group was supplemented by younger musicians filling voids left by those who had died or could no longer perform. The stage was dominated by a large, aged, black singer with a stubble beard, clad in a floor-length frock coat and wide-brimmed black hat, and who moved to the music. He exuded charisma through his pores. His mahogany hands were fielder's gloves that plucked the staccato rhythms from the ambient air. The famous Compay Segundo, on his *One Hundredth Birthday,* took the floor to dance with his wife. Later, a woman and her partner came forward. In black high heels with ankle straps, her skin was flan seen through a sheer film of caramel, her little *blue* dress was slit up the back to the top of her legs, with a row of sequins along one side seam. Her bare shoulders were gloveless gauntlets wrist to armpit, her lank charcoal hair appeared to be machete-trimmed, and her wide, smiling mouth reflected the spotlight from twinkling gold molars. She stepped and spun and swaggered and stretched and swayed and soared and swung and sauntered and stalked and slumped and stamped and shrugged and shuffled and shook. Mostly she pranced, with her spinal cord a puppet string tied to the "golden sticks" of a grand old Grammy Award winner as he struck the chrome rim of his snare drum. Even the most insecure women had no petty criticisms and rose to their feet along with the entire crowd. (One man fell; she had affected his inner ear.)

Returning to the Inglaterra terrace, we sat at tables of glazed tiles hand painted by fine Cuban artists and drank mojitos and natural daiquiris refortified with good rum leftover from the Tropicana. Two women who had managed to evade the security guards joined us at the table. They claimed to be twenty-one, but asked, "How old do you want us to be?"

One had soft, round features and a wealth of black ringlets. The other was her aesthetic counterpoint: angular, freckled, with cropped hair the color of wheatstraw; her father could have been named Ivan, her mother, Natasha. They giggled and laughed and teased about our inability to travel freely.

Around the corner, in the slum behind the hotel, a woman stands by the door of her casita, hoping to rent the floor of her dilapidated kitchen to a jinatera by the hour. There are four unmade beds in a room separated by a piece of gauze where once there was a door. She hopes and she waits. In Spanish, both words are the same: esperar.

To bed at 3:15 AM. Wake-up call at 3:45 AM. We fly through the dark to where all the plumbing functions properly and all the surfaces are smooth and clean. Where the glossy pages and the glowing plasma tell us that if you buy that product, your friends will envy you, your family will admire you, your lover desire you; you will be comfortable, healthy, and have a long life. If you are still bored or sad or lonely, you should have bought the more expensive model.

The chain is no longer drawn across the harbor at dark, but as the lights come up on El Morro fortress, the nightly cannon can be heard.

Each morning, on both sides of the Gulfstream, bitter seeds of discord are sown; and every night there is a harvest of frustration and despair.

"WE WILL IF WE HAVE TO"

When you cross that Rio Grande,
Boy, you in another country.

Texas Border Patrolman

THE MAYAN RUINS of Palenque are set into hillsides covered with a tropical forest and rise above a vast plain, beyond which lies the Pacific coast of southern Mexico. Although remote from the other three metropolises of the ancient empire, it draws determined travelers who seek out the rare and the beautiful. At dawn and dusk the lion-like roars of howler monkeys can be heard along the switchbacks leading up from the main road. A dramatic waterfall just behind the largest pyramid slakes the thirst of the jungle foliage.

The small town of the same name is a pleasant stop for tourists. To citizens of the republic, Chiapas—the name of the state—provokes deep emotions. It was here that social justice, the purported pride of the nation, was arriving three generations too late. The road to the ruins was blocked by a contingent of boy soldiers who would politely examine our passports each time we passed. Locals of all ages wore T-shirts with the image of Subcomandante Marcos. At the archaeological site, Lacandon men wearing floor length tunics of unbleached muslin, with hair to their waists, smoking homemade cigars, offered dolls wearing ski masks with tiny corncob pipes in the mouth holes. For ten years, the few remaining Lacandons had given refuge to the rebel leader and his men in the vast jungle surrounding the ruins of Bonampak, "until the people asked for their help." Only then did the hooded, pipe-smoking poet ride out of exile with his men.

In a Palenque restaurant a large mural depicts the sub-comandante (still hooded) at the accord table with federal officials. They no more knew his kind existed than did other capital residents seventy years before, when they woke to one thousand Zapatista campfires fogging the Paseo de Reforma. A sepia photo shows them breakfasting on rolls and coffee at the elite "House of Tiles," wearing wide sombreros and bandoliers, with rifles close at hand. One has a deep cheek scar and eyes glazed from puffing *"La Cucaracha."*

We paid a few pesos to camp beneath a grove of trees in a fenced area by the road. That night we walked to an outdoor bar and restaurant. Along the way Manuel showed up. There is always a "Manuel" or a "Xavier" or a "Gino," and their similarity is astonishing. He focuses his attention on a North American woman and proposes escorting her to special, little-known places. Of course, he wants her to visit his home and meet his family, especially his elderly mother. All of this will take place tomorrow or the next day. Tonight he does not have much money with him, and very reluctantly agrees to her paying for dinner, drinks, and whatever else he needs. It seems that the more intelligent and sophisticated the woman, the more vulnerable she is.

Manuel conversed with the bartender often. Tequila flowed like water. The air was cloudy with pungent smoke. At one point I struck the table with my machete for conversational emphasis. Some of us had the presence of mind to retire early. Beginning to doze, I was startled by the sound of one of the vans pulling away.

Pete answered my shout with the assurance that everything was all right; that some of them were going for a ride. I was told later of the reality: They had decided to have a midnight swim in the waterfall. There were many reasons this was imprudent. The most significant ones were cultural and legal: The ruins were sacred to the contemporary natives, as they were the dwellings of the old gods. Often ashes from burnt offerings of *copal* could be found on the stone platforms. The federal government protected the sites and prohibited entrance after dark. A group of loud, nude *gringos* cavorting among the shrines would offend religious sensibilities and violate secular law.

As the vehicle approached the gates, someone exclaimed, "There are the guards!" Another answered, "Fuck 'em!" One of the women piped up, "We will if we have to." Her reply became our slogan.

As luck would have it, it was Mexico's Independence Day. The small park office was closed and dark. There were no soldiers, only three elderly men at one side of the table facing the entrance drive. They all seemed to be in a stupor. One's head was cradled in his arms next to an empty bottle that was probably payment for relieving the regular sentries for the holiday celebration. An antique rifle lay on the concrete stoop. There was not even a blink of acknowledgement as the unlit van rolled quickly by.

At first light I was awakened by shouts and curses. Every pack left outside the tents was gone. The campground owner met us with the news that Manuel had been arrested the night before while hitchhiking with three of the packs stacked on the road shoulder beside him. The gear was in the gatehouse and Manuel was in the Palenque jail. Pete suggested we go there and "interrogate" him.

Within the municipal building, the Police Chief's desk sat in an open cloister facing the central patio. Pete explained the situation and another officer led us to a windowless, unpainted concrete block structure that might have been a one-car garage. The overhead door was unlocked and raised to reveal a massive wood grille with hundreds of small openings that could have dated back to the conquest. The smell of human waste hit us from the dark void just before thirty fingers wormed through the holes. Eyes appeared. Two were Manuel's, and they were crying. He sobbed that it was not him but a Guatemalan who had been the thief, and begged that we take him to help find the lost equipment. Pete looked at the jailer, who just shook his head and slowly closed the door on the anguished pleading. Pete's face had gone pale and his manner was appreciably less aggressive. At camp the remaining packs had been located deep in the bushes.

~~~

Two nights later we dined in Campeche's Historic District at a restaurant that boasted butterfly shrimp "as big as your hand." From the end of the table one of the women asked when we planned to leave the next day. She had been joined by a handsome, well-dressed young man.

He had offered to show her around in the morning.

FLEA ON THE DOG

...I was born on the backseat of a Greyhound bus,
rolling down Highway 41.

Allman Brothers

A FTER NINE AND a half sleepless overnight hours, Buenos Aires to Miami, short on funds and long on time, I decide to take a Greyhound bus to Orlando. My limping left leg, stiffened from the flight, inflamed from Argentine red wine and red meat, curses me for a fool. My last long bus ride—twenty-four hours, Chicago to Coral Gables—is embossed in memory after fifty years.

I board a world of wonder and awe. Snobbishly contriving to avoid contact with other passengers, I become aware they are moving away from the unshaven, rumpled old guy who just sat down.

∽∽∽

Once upon a time I hitchhiked from Dubois, Wyoming, to Nashville, thirty-one rides: the first a nurse who asked me to camp a few days in the Wind River Range. (A sage once advised that if such an offer were declined, it would be regretted, "...maybe not the next day, or the next week, but eventually." He was right.) Shivering all night in the Sandias, I learned not to expect rides after dark but to find a dry place away from the road and put down my bag at twilight. Outside Oklahoma City, a VW van driver asked my destination: "I can't get you there, but I can get you high." A euphoric hour later, a jolly fat woman with two pretty daughters: "I don't generally pick up hitchers, but I told the girls, 'Now there stands a nice, God-fearin' young man.'" A couple in Arkansas: "Have a swig! We're celebratin'. Ike here just got out of the slammer." I arrived at my destination to find that the airport of The Country Music Capital of the World had closed at 10:00 PM. I slept on a bench outside until it opened.

<p align="center">~~~</p>

The bus is surprisingly clean and comfortable. Two employees coach the novice driver: "This time of day, get to the left before that light." One lectured the passengers on behavior like a homeroom teacher, and then chanted a litany of stops, informing that one could stay aboard and disembark in San Francisco. A dupe for feminine artifice, I was impressed by a new arrival with long eyelashes, a too tight T-shirt (reading "Give Peaches a Chance," with tiny fruit forming a heart), and a brilliant sleeve of flaming demon tattoos. The shifting of social strata that embraces body art is fascinating: from Edwardian royalty, to sailors, to rock stars, until now, when every woman not restricted by faith or family has emblazoned on her spine base Art Nouveau scrollwork, improbable butterflies, or terms of endearment: "Rocky's Road"[?!]. The driving coach refuses the newcomer one seat after another as being "reserved for crew," until she asks demurely, "How many asses have you got?!" A man braver than I takes the seat beside her, but he leans away for the entire journey. Another voluptian of indeterminate origins comes on in a faux-batik rayon dress as sheer as a whisper. She makes friends easily.

The busmen dub her "Miss Daytona," as in, "Miss Daytona, can you get those fellows to quiet down?"

Passing Delray Beach I reflect on recently canceling a luncheon invitation I had from an attractive realtor who lives there; also at the luncheon would be her fashion model daughter and her son-in-law, a famous novelist. If they could see me now...

A rider with handsome features that somehow bespeak a certain weakness moves down the aisle and into the beauty queen's magnetic field. At Melbourne he is ordered off the bus for smoking in the restroom. As he protests to the surrounding uniforms on the sidewalk, a woman hands a fifth in a plastic bag through the doorway: "This was left on the seat, but it ain't mine! I don't want to get kicked off the bus! I paid too much for the ticket."

After seven hours the driver misses the Orlando station entrance, and we lurch over the curb.

A tall, older African American in a wide-lapelled suit, amber granny glasses, and a white cowboy hat with "Cherokee" on the band has ridden alone. As he awaits his luggage, Miss Daytona approaches and writes down her cell phone number for him.

The Bank at Hanga Roa

I tell my friends, "It's certainly not normal."

Bonnie Bolt
Normal, Illinois

W HEN THE BRITISH finally found Tahiti, sailors from the slums of London were welcomed, literally with open arms, by the women of the island. Accustomed to paying for such favors, they soon found a portable, durable currency: nails. The women came to expect, and eventually demand, payment. Nails became so scarce the ships' carpenters could hardly keep planks together. Thus prostitution and free enterprise were established in paradise.

1,500 miles away and 243 years later, patrons gather at the bank on Rapa Nui. The tiny island is the most isolated human habitat on earth. Around the ATM are wet, longhaired men with longboards. A block away, high waves of the cola-bottle–green glass of your childhood, say "shh!" when they hit the rocks. There are two certainties on Rapa Nui: You will not hear a cross word, and the machine, regardless of logos, will not accept your cards. It only dispenses to those it knows and loves. The clean, air-conditioned interior is enclosed by a contemporary structure. Children are everywhere. The dominant group is two to five year olds. One little boy pulls himself to the top of the teller line, a Herculean feat. Another climbs from an absent officer's chair to her desktop. All have stacks of brochures, either with ducklings (advertising credit cards) or Snoopy (MetLife). A toddler has made a nest of them for her doll and covered it with a Pooh blanket, while her sister fans it to sleep. Beautiful young women in translucent *pareus* pass to and fro. "Warriors" stand silently and proudly: Every warm surface has been tattooed. Women greet with cheek kisses, men with a complex sequence of handshakes. They smile and chat as if they had not seen each other only hours before. One stands out: a large Samoan woman who is visiting the island. Her body is covered wrists to ankles by a floor length dress. A stiff straw hat covers her head. When Saint Paul wrote to the Corinthians, he did not know his message would dictate what the Samoans would wear thousands of years later (missionary zeal gone awry). Tourists are in a line marked: "Foreign Currency Exchange," "Pregnant Women," "Invalids," and "Those of the Third Age." The visitors are a defensive lot, suspecting intricate schemes to defraud them of their dollars and euros. A woman wakes her Dalmatian and starts for the door. It is noon. The business day is over. Everyone had a good time and looks forward to seeing each other there tomorrow.

COLORS

...in Greece landscape and light are so beautiful,
so all-present, so intense, so wild,
that the relationship is immediately love-hatred,
one of passion.

The Magus
John Fowles

C LOUDS SPED TOWARD *viewers at the San Francisco "art theater" as repetitive, insistent music, like an Irish reel relieved by Arabic quarter-tones, preluding the credits announcing Anthony Quinn in the role he was born to play, and introducing me to the most beautiful place I have ever known.*

It is defined by colors, mostly primaries rendered pure and intense by the clear dry air, as though your visual acuity was amplified. Their brilliance is almost more than the eye can bear.

The Aegean Sea rolling by our charted motor-sailer, the *Annoula,* was royal blue, almost the indigo of new jeans, and topped by stark white wavelets: the colors of the Greek flag.

Of the seven islands in the Cycladic, or circular, archipelago, selected for us by an architect who lived there for thirteen years, each had a cultural personality of its own.

The shallow draft of our vessel allowed entrance to the harbor of tiny Kea, shaped like a woman's breast: a farming village at the nipple, a fishing village tucked into the base. At the taverna a woman wearing a T-shirt captioned "A woman needs a man like a fish needs a bicycle" berated the local men for dominating their women (based upon her twenty-four hours spent on our boat). The men's wind-burnt faces smiled as pipe smoke rose around caps that bespoke their maritime careers. They feigned an inability to understand and rode out the rant like a storm.

The church at Tinos could be seen from far offshore. A closer sighting revealed dark green trees adorning its bare seaward wall bearing pebbled-skinned yellow lemons as large as young mangoes. A street ascended from the town to the shrine, its cobbles bloodied each Holy Week by the knees of penitent pilgrims as they agonized their slow way up the hill.

A slate gray mound on the horizon became Mykonos, island of sun and flesh, the world capital of decadent self-indulgence. One-man fishing boats, painted bright colors, bobbed in the bay like children's toys. At a small beach young women husked off last night's little black dresses, changed into bikini bottoms, and waded into the clear water, while their lovers rolled over on the blankets for a little more sleep. Across the street a jeweler displayed a ring set with a square-cut stone almost the size of a domino tile. Asked if it was real, the shop owner declared, "We only sell *real* diamonds!" Six cafes face the water: a hundred shaded outdoor tables. Greek men sit in the back drinking muddy Turkish coffee and fingering worry beads. Tourists sip the fiery Ouzo, knowing not what they do. Every Mediterranean culture produces a version of the licorice tasting liqueur; the most notorious is France's absinthe, illegal in the United States because an ingredient, wormwood, is thought to "rot the brain." I avoid all of them, along with snakes, vicious dogs, and a certain type of woman.

At the far end of the harbor stands the Mariner's Chapel. Asymmetrical, biomorphic, the small structure seems made of melted sugar and is one of the most photographed religious structures of its size. The buildings are blindingly white, freshly painted, as required by law each spring; shutters, stair rails, and doors lacquered dark blue, or occasionally burnt sienna like dried blood, counterpoint their walls. They are contiguous, and flow with rounded corners and arches, like the Pueblos of our Southwest. The lanes are so narrow they prohibit vehicular traffic. They form a labyrinth and sometimes end in a private garden or on a rooftop, or more often, back where they started. Drunk, in the early morning hours, one could become lost forever, and, turning a corner, come face to bill with a giant pelican as tall as your shoulder with webbed feet the size of placemats, glaring at you for disturbing its sleep. It is one of the famous Pink Pelicans of Mykonos. When some of them died, Jacqueline Kennedy Onassis donated more of the unique, flamingo-colored birds to the island. A C-shaped thoroughfare defines the area restricted to pedestrians. Rental motor scooters fly by like angry hornets. There are daily sightings of casts and crutches.

Up a steep street is a fifteen-room hotel with a vine-covered terrace that looks over the village to the sea beyond. The owner, Mr. Nazos, hugs me and barely touches my neck with the traditional kiss. He is a tall courtly man, wearing a mischievous smile and a fisherman's cap. When we disagreed over room costs he said, "Let's use your figures, friends are more important than money." His wife extends her large arms to draw me to her ample bosom then brings out trays of Heineken and glasses of homemade wine. George, their handsome son, is sleeping off a night of entertaining a woman from France, or Germany, or The Netherlands. When women from our group return at 2:00 AM he will teach them traditional Greek dances on the terrace. I hope his shy sister, Sofia, will appear sometime.

Afternoon silence falls over the island as all take to their beds. A strong breeze plays with the sheers flanking the open window of our pristine, sparsely furnished room. A packet of sage wrapped in twine and a single goldfish in a clear unadorned sphere are on an end table. A lotus blossom light fixture with cream-colored petals hangs from the ceiling by a chain. She leans against me; her mouth moves down leaving a thin thread of moisture that disappears in the warm dry air.

We all walk down past the squat white windmills with conical thatched roofs. Tiny triangular sails turn the ancient wooden worm gears inside. Geraniums bleed around their bases. Down to "Little Venice," where water laps onto the street ends and slaps spume high above the seawall. Up the outside stairs to the wraparound balcony of The Verandah: We are lucky to find seats. A young waitress I have known for years kisses my cheek for photos while my companion frowns into her menu. From inside, dramatic music floods over us. The western sky is a smear of apricot that changes to fiery red-orange veined with cloud-wisps, then concentrates into a huge drop of blood and sinks into the sea. A moment of awed silence is followed by thousands of hands applauding up and down the waterfront. We sip expensive fancy drinks, such as the Black Pearl, all with fruit or flowers spilling over the rims. At the Caprice a semi-circle of glass frames a wraparound window seat pillowed in turquoise. It faces a table supporting a flower arrangement five feet tall. Our friend backs his wide buttocks into the arrangement, which topples to the floor, as the stricken bartenders shriek like schoolgirls.

It is now full dark and the show has begun. The lanes, brightly lit by shop windows, are filled with a parade of peacock people. In the occasional chapel burgundy votive candles animate the staring faces of icons and their perfectly concentric halos. Fresh fish, octopi, and prawns rest on a bed of cracked ice in front of Stavros'. On a corner under the stars its tables afford a view of hundreds of passersby: muscular men holding hands wearing only gold chains and Speedo bathing suits, women in transparent clothes that invite looking up, down or through. "Mohammad created silk so that women could go naked in public." We dine on dips of fish roe, whipped garlic, and onions and cucumbers chipped into yoghurt as we await lamb shanks or grilled lobsters. The salad vegetables have ripened on the island, the herbs are from nearby fields.

A chorus of men's voices fills the festive street. The crowds fall silent. Soon a funeral procession passes, with Mr. Nazos, his head raised in song, taking long strides just before the coffin. Later, while offering my condolences, he explained that the deceased woman had lived to over one hundred years. Sweeping his arm back in a gesture that took in everything in sight he said, "Look around you, why would she want to leave?"

Adolescents perform frenzied dances under strobe lights in the Scandinavian Bar. A crowd made up of only men wait in front of another entrance. One is wearing a red cape, pantyhose, cowboy boots, and a holstered pistol, *nada mas,* nothing more, as the Spanish say. Joe's is still selling *souvlaki,* skewers of cubed pork, lamb, or swordfish, and the shops are still open at 3:00 AM—it's a time for impulse buys. (Returning home, I unpacked yards of blue and white cloth. The mystery unfolded to become a four-foot by eight-foot Greek flag.)

Mid-morning finds you and your companion on a motor scooter tour. A web of bad roads connects beaches with names like Paradise and Super Paradise, each catering to specific sexual preferences.

There is a restaurant that has no name at the end of a rough narrow road overlooking a small, secluded bay of clear water, where a few swim nude while awaiting the opening. The hours are 1:00 to 3:00 PM but you can be served Boutari, the great white wine, over the gate until then. There are eight tables shaded by a trellis supporting grape vines. Inside the little building is a display of complex salads from which to choose, while on the terrace an elderly chef grills fresh fish, octopi, and two-inch-thick pork chops. A yacht or two are sometimes moored offshore while their owners walk up the path for lunch.

If this is not Paradise, where is it?

It may be on Santorini.

We have taken the large, comfortable ferry, as private vessels are sometimes prohibited passage during high summer winds. All are out on the port side. What seem to be two low hills on the horizon slowly becomes the crater rim of a mammoth, submerged ancient volcano. As we enter the break there is silence. There is no more wind. All are quiet, awestruck by the thousand-foot cordovan cliffs that encircle us, topped by white villages that look as tiny as baby teeth. We ride donkeys led by drovers up hundreds of switchback steps from the port to the town of Fira, then a short way beyond to the community of Firastefani and a café on the roof of a small hotel.

The view is startling. I know of no more dramatically beautiful place anywhere.

The branch manager of the National Bank of Greece and his charming wife manage the hotel for his father, who along with his uncle and their vast families own most of the restaurants, hotels, and apartments that spill down toward the edge of the precipice. Over the left sidewall is a tiny dwelling in total ruin opening onto a small terrace. The property was purchased a few years ago for over a million dollars, and soon resold for considerably more. The manager's brother hopes one day to become its owner. We are the only guests for a special wine party and are served mini-loaves of hard, dark bread and sophisticated appetizers, along with the first cherry tomatoes of summer. The sun dissolves into the mist of the heated crater far below, then reappears as a gigantic shimmering red ball before dropping into the sea. There are tears, even some sobs. We are overwhelmed.

There are those who claim the *Rambles* of Barcelona is the "most beautiful walk in the world." They have not strolled along the cliff tops descending into Fira. Domed chapels and churches and the terraces of homes and cafes all overlook the bay. With every turn the vantage changes. The cobbles turn sharply around the corner of Zafora's restaurant, with only a low wall and the sea beyond. A wedding ceremony is taking place on the lane, not an impromptu affair, but with a groom in tails and a bride in veils and a crowd of polished and preening guests. There is no cathedral that can compete with the setting.

Jewelry stores line the streets of Fira. Pretty women who know nothing of the products are employed to stand in the shop doorways and beckon husbands to bring their wives inside. At breakfast a building contractor who could have been an aging John Wayne told of how accommodating a shop owner had been. Having been asked his favorite liquor, a bottle of Jack Daniel's, a pitcher of water, and pail of ice appeared by his chair as if by magic. Shortly after recounting the story for us, his wife stepped into the dining room, literally dripping with gold, "like a ship bound for Tarsus."

Another man declined to say what he paid for his wife's braided gold necklace, thicker than her thumb, but he said his recent phone calls had been to determine if some property in Guatemala had been sold before making the purchase.

On the side streets there are shops with products of lesser elegance.

Si was a Central Florida county commissioner. With a crocodile smile and crocodile eyes, when he placed his hand on your shoulder you were in trouble. You knew he was lying, and he knew that you knew he was lying. *Although a charmer and a charlatan, it must be said that he had come through with an act of loyalty and endurance on the Inca Trail in Peru, for which we will always be grateful.* He combed his bleached blond hair across his bald dome and sprayed it with Aqua Net so that he could bob up from the surf with every strand in place. He was always plotting to separate twenty-year-old Kathy from her overly protective parents. At a tacky souvenir shop he hastily suggested they look at the wonderful displays; "Kathy and I will meet you later." The gods played a joke on Si: The gullible mother and father found the store filled with nothing but reproductions of acrobatic sex acts, from the classic erotic vases of antiquity to contemporary photos, graphically detailed, as playing card illustrations.

Just down the steps from the art galleries of central Fira is Franco's, well known to international travelers. It was selected by *Newsweek* as one of the Ten Best Bars in the World. The view of the crater below is *almost* comparable to that of our small hotel. On our first visits, women of wealth and position could be seen sunning themselves, stripped to their "small clothes." Larger now, with prohibitions on cell phones and cigars, delicate snacks are on offer, along with outrageously wonderful drinks, such as the Maria Callas, named after the opera diva whom Aristotle Onassis would escort there. He said something to the effect that, "I *own* an island. Unfortunately it is not Santorini!" Bringing it all back to reality, the drovers tether the donkeys a few tiers below, where they carpet the wide steps with manure.

One winter I rented a beautiful "cave dwelling," just below the hotel, with sixteen-foot-high vaulted ceilings that opened onto a large terrace overlooking the sea. The weather was milder than expected, except for brief afternoon rains that chilled to the bone. The dormant volcano below provided ample warmth as heat filtered up through the porous scree. Each morning I would walk up and down the steps to the harbor, have a draft at the Rendezvous, buy an *International Herald Tribune* and some canned goods, and return home.

Ostensibly, I was there to write, but the dramatic surroundings and the simplicity of my days led to a tranquil, introspective state. I scribbled not a word.

As I was one of very few foreigners at that time of year, the island's residents considered me their guest. Although Christian to the core, some Middle Eastern attitudes are integral in the Greek culture: Guests bring honor and an obligation to the hosts. I was treated as though I was born there and made welcome by everyone.

Having grown up where tourist exploitation is a mainstay of the economy, I suspected a commercial aspect to the invitation to New Year's Eve at the Rendezvous, but I was the only guest other than the staff and their families. On the small terrace the celebration began with the annual shearing of the bartender's hair and the shaving of his scalp. A table had been brought in that filled the interior room, allowing just enough perimeter space for chairs. Its broad surface was covered with festive foods. Drinks were handed from the bar. People I hardly knew had provided a home for the holidays.

Up the street is Mama's. Stepping inside the breakfast restaurant you are greeted with, "Mama loves you babies!" The meals are good and inexpensive, but the attraction is Mama. She is short, chubby, and always smiling as she moves among the tables embracing patrons with her large arms and shouting, "Safe sex!" "Where have you been? I heard you sailed in two days ago," and, "When are you going to bring Mama an American millionaire?!" Some of the best attractions are not on the Internet.

The art colony of Oia at the northern tip of the island encompasses galleries of fine paintings, shops of Byzantine jewelry and Oriental rugs, and an elegant restaurant with no sign other than a tile by the door depicting a snail over the words "Slow Food."

The elbow of the island is a mammoth stone monolith topped by ancient Roman ruins. Two black sand beaches flank it. At this time of year, only the heads of blond Nordics dot the cold waves. A narrow twisting path meanders down the inner wall of the crater to Red Beach with geothermal heated water, appealing to all.

On the shallow outer slopes the fertile volcanic soil is covered by apple-green grapevines, growing as wreaths on the ground to resist the wind.

Only a mile or so of the estimated five-mile length of Akrotiri has been excavated. Several millennia ago a cataclysmic eruption caused tidal waves around the world while burying the ancient city, along with its homes and art works, including intact murals depicting the denizens' way of life. Other images are accurate representations of the large animals of Equatorial Africa, thousands of miles away. Many believe it to have been the ancient Lost City of Atlantis.

∾∾∾

Somewhere away from the villages a small house overlooks the sea. It's where my heart lives.

The Song of Kathmandu

There is a song of Kathmandu,
Heard by many,
Known to few,
With a brang and a brong
And a cling, clang, cling;
And a tiny, timid, timorous ting.

THE HYENA COUGH and growl of scootercabs, little claustrophobic cowled vehicles; cheap rides through the madding crowd. From the airport you pass everything the imagination has ever screened in your most Technicolored dreams: small shops, small alleys, small dirt lanes alive with people. On the backs of motorcycles women in silk saris so brilliant they seem lit from within lean demurely on their little Himalayan Marlon Brandos, who sport thin moustaches and yellow-lensed Ray-Bans.

Now comes the sacred cow, The Goddess of Wealth (not a symbol, but her actual Royal Heiferness), stepping through strips of foil tea packets hanging from the doorhead and into the shop. The lady backs away. Even the child backs away as a thin string of green drips from the pink muzzle onto the scratched glass countertop. The bored bovine lunges awkwardly back into traffic, leaving behind a hot, wet, nonrefundable deposit over the scattered compact disks on the concrete floor.

There is brick dust and dirt dust and dust that lives in every piece of cloth; and exhaust smoke, and crematory smoke; and each early morning and evening, smoke from a thousand cooking fires.

As you penetrate Thamel, sound and color runs riot: store-faces flash and change, carpets and carvings, hanging clusters of crazed four-faced puppets, brassbound wooden Tibetan tea jugs, a multitude of Hindu gods, overbearing with their many arms, crowding the gentle Buddha. He knows not hurt, but his adherents do, each year as those of the other faith lead every male animal (the females having been impregnated), from housecats to water buffaloes, to decapitation as a bloody public sacrifice. Keeping the bell lever depressed on the ten-rupee rental bike, the cobbles ring it for you. Darkness is not allowed to take the streets. Every window glares, including that of the supermarket where a young mother begs milk for the infant on her arm. The mean-spirited confide that she sells it back for cash. (I hope she does, and I hope the nay-sayers rot in hell.) If you slip down an alleyway between the metalworkers' niches, the light goes away, leaving you in the dark hall of a huge house. The floor creaks. There is a sigh and a moan. The darkness becomes absolute. No one within fifteen thousand miles knows where you are. A tethered goat bleats as you emerge into a lantern-lit yard. The corner jewelry store displays black sapphires. The double stars shine from deep within the smooth drops of night. No one knows of what they are made.

No one knows.

No one knows.

In and Out of the Himalaya

*A stone's throw out from either hand
From that well-ordered road we tread,
And all the world is wild and strange...*

*For we have reached the Oldest Land
Wherein the Powers of darkness range.*

From the Dusk to the Dawn
Rudyard Kipling

ALL BUILDINGS BRISTLED around the Hong Kong airport, which seemed cantilevered over the sea. I avoid the large cities of Europe which have almost as many Jiffy Lubes and KFC's as Detroit and Des Moines, but Hong Kong was a *perro diferente* as the Mexicans say: a different dog. Views of the harbor were obscured by stacks of containers bound for everywhere. The clean streets pulsed with vitality. Shops displayed treasures of ancient and modern oriental art. Beautiful women rode public transport alone with knees and hands pressed together and eyes downcast.

Our hotel café was furnished in lacquered black Art Nouveau; the bedrooms were spacious. Ellen commented that there were a lot of doors opening and closing all night, and that our rooms were made up each time we ventured out.

Ellen had done a few things.

I had met her briefly, to give architectural advice about her condominium complex on the Florida coast. Five years later she called to say that since the death of her husband, who owned

179

an international construction company, she had continued to travel and now, along with her son, wanted to go places with us. She was slight of build, soft spoken, and a lady in the best sense of the word. Modest to a fault, she revealed her adventures reluctantly. She had been a bush pilot in Equatorial Africa, ice-climbed major peaks, and was once incarcerated in Brazil with twelve of her husband's male employees. She laughed about the men's main topics of conversation being, in descending order, the condition of their bowels, sports, and *then* women. A local tabloid noted that her belt buckle depicted a skull and crossbones. Ellen had won annual solo air races from Miami to Managua. She still flies her Tiger Moth. Recently, she said she was going skiing with her adult granddaughter. When I said she would be doing the same thing with her great-granddaughter she replied, "Probably so!"

In Hong Kong she liked to breakfast at the Peninsula Hotel, whose guests are transferred from the airport in Rolls-Royces.

Our first night, we sought out Pinky's Tattoo Parlor in the Wan Chai district, made famous by "The World of Susie Wong." My friend Scott was probably the only U.S. naval officer to leave the service with a large cobra decorating each bicep. Pinky had been the artist, but we found that he had moved to Beverly Hills to illustrate the skin of famous movie stars. His brother was still in business at the top of the stairs. After I ingested a Valium and two scotch and waters, he needled a thumb-sized image of a serpent on my right buttock. Even with the nest of flames that was added in New Zealand, it looks like nothing more than a small bruise.

At the spa, under the same ownership as our hotel, three of us were given terrycloth robes, paper sandals, and locker keys. After a workout with free weights, we showered in pristine marble stalls with shampoo, liquid soap, and moisturizer for each user. We plunged into first the hot pool, then the cold pool, and then showered again. In the sauna we consumed the pineapple slices warmed by the hot stones. An attendant grimaced disgustedly as he took away the rinds. The Cantonese man beside us said the fruit was there for fragrance. We had eaten the air freshener! As I lay down, a muscular man placed his feet under my armpit and pulled from the waist, then stretched each leg in the same manner. He sluiced me with warm suds, then commenced to exfoliate my skin, periodically showing the filth he had rubbed off. After another shower we were wrapped in velour blankets. Reclining in loungers equipped with headphones, we watched images of landscapes change on the wall. We were asked if we wanted one or two masseuses. The massages had no sexual aspects, except that the pretty women, being short, had to rub their pubic areas against the tops of our heads to reach some areas. We were shown a menu of additional services including a haircut, shave, ear clean, and eye clean. *Eye clean?!*

I felt better than I had in years. The entire morning cost US$45.

In the hotel lobby I commented on the well-dressed Asian couples without luggage checking in with the women's electronic card. A receptionist explained, "Chinese women. You like Chinese women?" I showed the business card to the cabbie and five of us were on our way. At least a dozen other taxis were lined up at a three-story building, part of an impressive shopping mall. A wide red carpet flowed to the curb from a landing where a uniformed and armed man sat at a desk marked: Security. Four greeters in 1950s style prom dresses holding walkie-talkies seemed embarrassed as one apologetically explained that we could not be admitted in shorts and tennis shoes. We sped to the hotel and were back in a flash. Perhaps fifty tables surrounded a twenty-foot by twenty-foot dance floor. Sixteen pretty violinists in top hats, tails, and tights provided music for a performance by ballroom dancers. We were informed that we were only obligated to pay for our drinks, but we could beckon over any of the women in slit dresses. They would start a timer. We could ask them to leave at any time. None of us chose a partner (virtue by way of limited finances) except one, who chatted with an English woman who owned a lingerie shop and worked here two or three nights a week. She gave us a tour. On the third level there were private rooms with etched glass fronts, where groups of young Asian businessmen sat with hostesses. She explained that there were three hundred women employed and that at any given time about two hundred were on out calls. Our hotel was owned by a syndicate that controlled twelve such places; there were five syndicates operating in Hong Kong. She charged my friend US$300 to spend the night. Unless my math is flawed, this indicates about eighteen thousand women earning around US$5,400,000 per night, thus explaining the solitary women on public conveyances.

~~~

Boarding the Royal Nepal flight to Kathmandu, the crew welcomed us with praying hands and a murmured *"Namaste."* An approximate translation is: "I acknowledge the goodness within you."

The gates of the Kathmandu Guest House open to the center of Thamel. As you pass in, an old guard in a rumpled uniform comes to attention giving a palm-out salute. There are a couple of rafting and bicycling offices, then a courtyard with tables flanked by fountains and small shrines. To the left of the entrance are the US$5 rooms. Just inside, half a dozen members of the family that owns the establishment crowd behind a small counter. They seem to record nothing, yet hundreds from all over the world pass through daily. All payments are made in Nepali rupees, which can be purchased from a teller's window across the room. Backpacks are stacked in a pyramid, and their owners stand around awaiting transport. In the afternoons a woman attends an unmarked desk to arrange tours across Tibet or to a nearby village. A shallow glass case displays faxes, some yellowed and fading, scrolled and thumb-tucked to indicate the recipient's name. A message read: "I enjoyed being with you last night. I will be in Goa, India, from April 14 – 26. Please try to meet me there." Now some guests spend entire days hunched over computer keyboards oblivious to the life outside passing them by. A couple of women in native dress, on their hands and knees, sweep the marble floor with cloths as big as carpets. The wide corridor leads to the "Standard" rooms at US$15. The "Garden Facing" rooms cost US$20 and look out on a lawn surrounded by sitting areas shaded by citrus trees. A painted Buddha placidly watches over the tranquil scene. There are always a couple of European women sunning as much skin as modesty allows. They are there to drive a young man, returning from three weeks in the mountains, out of his mind.

One guest complained that his perimeter room looked onto a private yard where a man was mesmerizing cobras. He was moved to another with a view of a family slaughtering a goat.

One early morning I left my camera, thinking there would be nothing worth photographing. At the gates a huge elephant and his mahout passed by on their way to work.

An hour before closing, a crowd forms at the next-door bakery to buy the day's products at half price. The bargains entail a risk, as some of the perishables have not been refrigerated.

Down the street are vegetarian restaurants, cavernous bookstores with treasures of Eastern philosophy, shops selling knockoffs of designer travel clothing and gear, surprisingly durable for the price, and a store with every type of Gurkha knife ever issued, complete with historical notes and polished wood display stands.

I think I misunderstand the voice yelling, "Condor! Condor!" Pablo Segovia waves down from a roof terrace. This is the third country we have encountered each other in during the past year. Once was at the First Pass on the Inca Trail in Peru, with both of us guiding trekkers. The second was in his wonderful hometown of Mendoza, Argentina, where he had procured guides for our first attempt on Aconcagua. *Our staff and their wives joined us for a farewell dinner at an elegant restaurant that served good red wine at seventy-five cents a glass, and steaks as thick as telephone books. Crazy Harry had told some rather crude jokes, and I wondered how I would create a diversion. A girlfriend who crossed from Cuba when she was twelve had taught me that Spanish verbs, such as* comer *("to eat"), can be altered to indicate one who does the act to excess, such as in* comelón *("a glutton"). When I ordered a second steak, declaring that I was a* comelón, *our guests became quiet. I ordered an additional baked potato, repeating loudly that I was a* comelón, *and the dining room fell silent. Pablo then told the table about he and I meeting two women on my previous visit. I was surprised at his indiscretion in narrating what had ensued. Before I could call out a desert order, Pablo touched my sleeve and whispered, "Condor, in Argentina a* comelón *is a man who eats other men." Ah, yes, smooth indeed.*

In Thamel, Pablo and I made our way to the Rum Doodle restaurant and bar, named after a fictitious peak in a humorous novel. Climbing groups dined while seriously planning going up, or celebrated coming down. The walls were covered with stylized silhouettes of "yeti footprints" signed by individuals and teams. The area behind the bar was reserved for those who had achieved Mount Everest (29,029 feet). Photos of Tenzing Norgay and Sir Edmund Hillary, each draped with the traditional white scarf, had pride of place. Rienhold Messner had signed one footprint; three toes had been torn away, reflecting his loss to frostbite in the Andes. Later there would be signatures of the teams on which many lives were lost attempting to summit during the tragic year of 1996. Only a dry soul would not be moved.

At the Kathmandu airport we waited for the klaxon horn to sound, indicating that the weather was clear enough for the forty-five–minute flight between there and Lukla. The short take-off and landing Otters lined up on the tarmac to lift off within seconds of each other. We flew parallel to the great white wall of the high Himalaya, then through a narrow slot in a ridge, with trees at the wingtips. A deep gorge dropped under us and then, far below, a dirt strip about 100-yards long *sloped* down to its edge. Planes were passing in the air. On landing the small aircraft would turn, disgorge its passengers, take on more, rev its engines and bump down the runway until it fell away below. Once airborne, the pilot and co-pilot would give each other a high-five. Now and then, like a large foil slug, a shiny hyperbaric bag cocooned a trekker with altitude sickness as he or she awaited evacuation.

Lukla, the trailhead for those going into the Khumbu region, has been a boomtown for years. The wooden walks lining the mud streets are extended yearly to accommodate more small hotels and restaurants. This is the land of Sherpas, devout Buddhists. We have left Hinduism behind, with its caste system that preordains who, by accident of birth, would spend their lives cleaning toilets. "Sherpa" originally designated the ethnic group living among the mountains of Northeast Nepal. It became carelessly misused to mean "porter" because of so many that served early expeditions in that capacity. It also indicates a rank within the trekking staff (similar to that of sergeant) that insures the porters, cooks, and kitchen boys efficiently execute the Sirdar's (leader's) requests. They also monitor the client's wellbeing.

To call the Sherpa people noble is an injustice. They *live* the Buddhist philosophy, taking joy in every journey and every task, regardless of how arduous. Their hypersensitivity to the feelings of others is incredible. They love life and its every aspect gives them happiness.

Our staff initially numbers about twenty for the dozen of us. About half will be periodically paid and discharged as we consumed the food cargo. Our packs are consolidated into parcels of thirty kilos (sixty-six pounds), thirty pounds for each of two trekkers and six pounds for the porter. The loads are packed into open, cone-shaped wicker baskets with shoulder straps. The porter's only other gear is a T-shaped walking stick, against which they rest briefly before ascending the steepest slopes. Some are barefoot.

Nawang, our Sirdar, is the son of a famous guide. Although he is well schooled in all the details, we are his first group, and he is deeply aware of his responsibilities. He likes to improve his English by asking about nuances, such as the difference between "blossom" and "bloom." His assistant, Thawang (also a guide's son) is somewhat less sophisticated, thus more vulnerable to mischievousness. I overheard him practicing a proclamation one of us had prompted him to announce: "Let's make lak yak sheet, and heet the trail!"

We weave through villages, under prayer flags and around *mani* walls of flat stones carved with religious mantras. Even porters carrying atrocious double loads for a few rupees greet us with *Namaste!* The people are small with delicate features. Even the very elderly women are handsome. Many are orna-mented with heavily encrusted gold facial jewels. One type is a chain with droplets, connecting a lobe plug to a nostril ring. A Floridian says they look like bass plugs. Occasionally an "apple house" appears in a leafy orchard. The scent of baking fruit wafts up the trail. Those who do not drink alcohol fall on the fritters, pies, and tarts, lathered with jams and jellies, with a ferocity that is startling in order to get their body's necessary level of sugar. We sleep in unfurnished plank rooms. Heat seeps into those near the kitchen along with a fog of smoke. The cooks carry live chickens slung over their wrists, part of an unsuccessful effort to provide Western food. Ellen suggests I ask them to prepare their traditional dishes. With that, the meals become delicious.

Bridges are suspended high above rushing rivers. Two cables provide handholds and support plank steps. Invariably some are missing. If one crosses alone it is not too daunting. If others mount the swaying structure, especially if they are leading beasts of burden, a focus of will is required.

A sheer wall appears above the confluence of two rivers. An appreciable increase in altitude is somewhat facilitated by the shallow zigzag trail up the face. The decrease in ambient oxygen has its effect. We stopped to talk to a man wearing a U.S. flag patch and two lean, muscular women in long India-print skirts. I asked where they had been: "Everest." "The Base Camp?" "No, the summit." One of them was the first American woman to conquer the mountain. A couple of years later we ran into the man and a friend in Mendoza after they had just accomplished Aconcagua as the last of their "Seven Summits" (each continent's highest peak). Our meeting was coincidence enough, but the tale they told was even more extreme. I guess they had thought us an odd bunch. Remembering my name, when the American Ambassador erroneously congratulated their members who had not succeeded, they replied, "No sir, we climbed Mount Donahoo!" The incident was so incredible that I asked them to verify the story in writing.

At the top of the ascent a crude wooden building exhibits a sign in rough brush strokes: "Everest Tea House." Before us rises Namche Bazaar, the last town, an amphitheater of small hotels, shops, and restaurants on terraced lanes, facing down the valley, with mammoth white peaks in the background. The only way in is on foot. Beyond, tiny settlements dot the footpath north. Japanese investors built a luxury hotel and a private air-strip. The sudden effects of high altitude caused serious trauma in the guests and the venture failed. Tibetan traders come down across snow-choked passes, the world's highest, bringing goods varying from sacks of salt to cut silk Chinese saddle blankets that would bring tens of thousands of dollars at Christie's. They sleep on the ground around a central shrine. They are friendly and innocent, yet their eyes have a light seen only of those of wild animals. Outdoor displays offer human skulls decorated with metal disks and semiprecious stones; art in brass, gold, and silver; a basket of raw turquoise nuggets, all for a pittance. One shop specializes in state-of-the-art climbing gear, recently sluffed off by expeditions coming down.

The Chinese owner of the hotel on our first trip and his Japanese mistress were disliked by the community. He knocked a boy down during our stay, claiming the lad startled him on the dark street. While I was taking an ice-water shower the villagers attacked our building, breaking all the windows with stones. I found the dining room locked from the inside with our group barricaded within. One man (there is *always* one) insisted we leave at once. Nawang and some of his staff arrived, their cool heads prevailed, and peace was restored.

On subsequent visits we lodged at an inn managed by Sherpa relatives of our trekking company owner. I made friends with Pemba, one of the cousins, and each year she presented me with the white scarf. Later I read that she became (by minutes) the second Nepalese woman to climb Mount Everest. More years passed and we heard she died on an ascent.

Nawang's mother invited us to her home. As the eldest male I was ceremoniously offered a bowl of yak butter tea, which I managed to keep down without gagging. That afternoon we paid off the last of our porters, putting two each of their loads on yaks. The short animals shaggy coats were better suited to resisting the cold of the region beyond than the porters' sparse rags. The yaks responded instantly to the drovers' whistles or voice commands. The men were friendly, but conversed only among themselves in what seemed to be another language.

Two women in native dress stood beside the path, negotiating in rupees. I noticed an American Express card in one of their wallets.

The trail became narrow and steeper. The settlements were made up of only a few thatched stone houses. Some provided our lodging. In one room a guide's wife would prepare meals over a primitive wood stove or an open fire, invariably wearing a wide smile decorated with gold teeth. The other area was a dormitory just large enough for an aisle and a low plank platform where a dozen or so could sleep side-by-side, head to feet for privacy. A loud fart or abrupt snore would cause the adjacent person to awaken with alarm.

Eventually we came to Gokyo. The turquoise lakes glowed. The sky was deep blue. A recent snow had covered the slopes running down to the valley. Colorful rugs hung drying on the lodge walls. The Tibetan border was five miles beyond. We were surrounded by some of the world's highest peaks: Gyachung (26,089 feet), Cho Oyu (26,906 feet), Lhotse (27,940 feet).

We had chosen Gokyo (15,984 feet) as the apex of our trek because of its views of Mount Everest. After an easy climb, we reached the summit at sunrise.

Lyle is brilliant, soft-spoken and modest, yet enthusiastic about any risk or challenge. Rita is spirited and mischievous. A psychologist in the personnel section of a large corporation, she often suggested we institute a screening questionnaire for those hoping to join us. The sun found Lyle and Rita in native dress, holding hands at the summit, enveloped by smoldering incense. Laurie stepped forward to read their wedding vows. Then a surprise: She announced a second ceremony. Chaz had proposed to Susan as they climbed in the dark. She accepted the jade ring he had brought from Hong Kong. Martha had decorated our lodge room with pink toilet paper streamers, with congratulatory phrases written in lipstick. Huddled around a small stove, we ate a gingerbread wedding cake prepared by our cooks.

We gathered for our farewell night at Lukla. Our staff sang Sherpa songs. Girls peeked through the windows, too shy to join in. Some worked as porters; while unable to carry the same loads as the men, their endurance was much greater.

None of our macho men *and women* took pictures of frail bodies laden with our large burdens.

Cash and excess gear were distributed as gratuities.

Nawang was so highly regarded that we pledged to underwrite the US$2,000 required for his application to the Hillary School.

He subsequently studied medicine in China. Lyle and Rita sent a stethoscope and a microscope.

Nawang returned to the hill country of his youth as the first Sherpa doctor.

"Dinero en Minutos": A Bad Day in Buenos Aires

*Western Union and its agents may decline
to accept or pay any money transfer...*

Western Union money transfer form

T HE OVERNIGHT FLIGHT from Miami was almost a pleasure:
good food (pasta dishes or unadulterated, grass-fed
beef), excellent wines, and movies that had not been
selected as pabulum for the mind. The journey was to provide
a Wine Harvest Festival excursion in Mendoza, Argentina,
for David and Susan, as compensation for our cancelling their
Guatemala adventure because of the swine flu scare. David is a
knowledgeable, retired military careerist, and Susan an enthusiastic and appreciative Midwesterner, to whom every new
experience outside the cornbelt is a revelation and a delight.
They, alone, would make up our traveling group.

Arriving in the morning, I anticipated a long layover in
Buenos Aires, but I decided to clear Immigration and Customs
early. I had only a few dollars left, but we had sent adequate funds
ahead, via Western Union, that I intended to retrieve in Mendoza.
The notice on the immigration booth window displayed the flags
of Australia, the United Kingdom, and the United States, and
declared that, as of a month before, citizens of these countries

must pay US$130.00 to enter Argentina. The levy was enacted in reciprocity for those nations' increasingly strict entry require-ments. I did not have the required amount. When informed of my situation, the ranking officer announced to all within earshot that she could not believe a *North American* would travel without excess cash, and that under no circumstances would I be allowed to pass without payment. The employees of Aerolinas Argentina were sympathetic (as they had not informed their ticket holders of the change).

Using a phone card, I attempted to call my daughter Dana, but no one answered. I reached our friend, Jon, to find he was with Dana at a hospital emergency room. Jon agreed to contact another friend who would wire additional funds to me in Buenos Aires. He later gave me the transfer code and said that there was a Western Union office at the nearby domestic terminal. With an escort, I was reluctantly allowed to go to the office. It was 12:30 PM on Saturday, and under the familiar yellow and black Western Union sign a notice showed that the branch closed at noon and would reopen Monday.

Ms. Immigration ordered me to be on the next flight to Miami, and the airline supervisor said that I must be at the gate in thirty minutes. I asked if I could fly back from Miami the next day, when David and Susan would arrive. I could, but would have to buy another ticket at around $1,000.00. I began to "sweat the big drop." Evading the supervisor, I went to the restaurant and passed from table to table, eventually finding four Australians willing to listen to me. (My pitch sounded like scams I had heard all over the world.) One of the Australians was skeptical, two were indifferent, while the fourth dropped 120 Australian dollars on the table. Another put down thirty dollars more, saying that should be sufficient.

Immigration refused payment as the money was not in U.S. currency. I went downstairs to the money exchange, again with an escort, to find that the double conversion yielded less than the sum required to enter the country. Back at the restaurant, the manager agreed to change my mound of notes for U.S. cash. I finally entered Argentina with two dollars left in my pocket, but I had missed the connecting flight to Mendoza.

Alex, a trusting cab driver, agreed to take me into the city, where I could retrieve my wired cash from another Western Union office. During the hour drive he mentioned that there had been a catastrophic earthquake in Santiago, Chile. The city was in chaos and the airport had been closed.

The Western Union office was in the beautiful suburb of Recoleta where, on a previous visit, I had watched tango dancers under the trees while sampling culinary delights. (Even now Argentina is the best-fed nation in the hemisphere, with the highest caloric consumption per capita.) In one restaurant were pictures of Juan Fangio, the racecar driver. One oil company markets Regular, High Test, and *¡Fangio!* It is a romantic country: Its heroes die hard. Across the way is Recoleta cemetery, a city of mausoleums, grandiose and sometimes bizarre. They occupy the most expensive real estate in the country. Narrow spiral stairs connect their levels. During the economic collapse, piles of bones could be seen making way for more prosperous families. Eva Peron was interred there, over the objections of the aristocracy. Military fraternities still place wreaths on the monument to a former dictator. Relatives of those tortured to death by his regime spit upon it.

The Western Union office turned out to be a small open counter at the intersection of two corridors in a new shopping mall. The attendant said he could not release payment to me because my middle name, as on my passport, had not been included in the transfer. He told me that another location, across town, could remedy the omission. After waiting in line at a Super Wal-Mart that handled Western Union transfers, I was told their computer system was not in service. I went to a telephone office and called Jon, still at the hospital with Dana.

He arranged to correct the omission of my middle name so that I could eventually get the money from Western Union.

Meanwhile, Alex treated me to a liter of Quilmes, the beer that sponsors the famous Boca Juniors soccer team, and confided the personality differences between his wife and his mistress. We tentatively planned a tango excursion for over New Years.

After Jon had corrected the omission of my middle name, I finally received the funds from Western Union. Alex took me to a modest hotel, and I agreed to pay any amount he thought fair. It was a sizeable sum. After a shower, clean sheets, and fresh clothes, I was on the hotel steps early the next morning waiting to return to the airport.

As they could not fly into Santiago to document the horrors of the earthquake, international journalists filled the Mendoza flight. The overheads were packed with camera equipment. I assured them their drive over the Andes from Mendoza would be safe and spectacular. A Canadian woman said she would have preferred to stay at the wine festival.

At the Hotel Aconcagua in Mendoza I was welcomed as though it was my home. The manager said David and Susan had not yet arrived, but their lodging had been prepared. From my room on the twelfth floor, I reached Dana by phone. I was relieved to hear that she was feeling better. She told me that David and Susan had left a message to say the Panama City-Santiago leg of their flights had been cancelled because of the earthquake.

They would not be coming.

≈≈≈

My hotel room window overlooked an endless carpet of treetops. For three days, until the next available flight home, I slept and read and read and read and slept and watched television (after the books ran out) and slept. Each night I would venture out for a meal at a sidewalk restaurant. The first began with *jamon serrano,* the best of which, in Madrid, is a costly substance like cocaine or gold, followed by a 480-gram *bife de chorizo,* a steak the size of a baby's head. This was accompanied by a hearts-of-palm salad, a bottle of mineral water, and a bottle of Malbec from a nearby winery (which the waiter discouraged, but which tasted like nectar to me). All of that, including the wine, cost less than a small family's order at their favorite fast food outlet.

The last night I could hear music from the Plaza Italia, a block away.

～～～

Several weeks after returning home, I received the following email:

Hi Buz,

Great to hear from you. I'm glad I could help and hope the remainder of your trip was more enjoyable! Western Union *would be the easiest way of transferring the cash. Can you forward to a location in Melbourne? Do you need more details? My contact details are listed in the email.*

Many thanks!
Gokhan
Melbourne, Australia.

Happy the man and happy he alone,
he who can call today his own:
he who secure within, can say,
Tomorrow do thy worst, for today I have lived.

John Dryden

www.ingramcontent.com/pod-product-compliance
Lightning Source LLC
Chambersburg PA
CBHW020507100426
42813CB00030B/3155/J